PICTURE YOURSELF DEVELOPING YOUR PSYCHIC ABILITIES:

Step-by-Step Instruction for Divination, Speaking to Spirit Guides, and Much More

TIFFANY JOHNSON

Course Technology PTR
A part of Cengage Learning

COURSE TECHNOLOGY
CENGAGE Learning™

Australia, Brazil, Japan, Korea, Mexico, Singapore, Spain, United Kingdom, United States

COURSE TECHNOLOGY
CENGAGE Learning™

Picture Yourself Developing Your Psychic Abilities: Step-by-Step Instruction for Divination, Speaking to Spirit Guides, and Much More

Tiffany Johnson

Publisher and General Manager, Course Technology PTR:
Stacy L. Hiquet

Associate Director of Marketing:
Sarah Panella

Manager of Editorial Services:
Heather Talbot

Marketing Manager:
Jordan Casey

Acquisitions Editor:
Megan Belanger

Project Editor:
Jenny Davidson

Technical Reviewer:
Jeff Belanger

PTR Editorial Services Coordinator:
Jen Blaney

Interior Layout Tech:
Shawn Morningstar

Cover Designer:
Mike Tanamachi

DVD-ROM Producer:
Brandon Penticuff

Indexer:
Sharon Shock

Proofreader:
Sara Gullion

Printed in the United States of America
1 2 3 4 5 6 7 11 10 09

© 2010 Course Technology, a part of Cengage Learning.

ALL RIGHTS RESERVED. No part of this work covered by the copyright herein may be reproduced, transmitted, stored, or used in any form or by any means graphic, electronic, or mechanical, including but not limited to photocopying, recording, scanning, digitizing, taping, Web distribution, information networks, or information storage and retrieval systems, except as permitted under Section 107 or 108 of the 1976 United States Copyright Act, without the prior written permission of the publisher.

For product information and technology assistance, contact us at

Cengage Learning Customer and Sales Support, 1-800-354-9706

For permission to use material from this text or product, submit all requests online at **cengage.com/permissions**

Further permissions questions can be emailed to **permissionrequest@cengage.com**

All trademarks are the property of their respective owners.
Library of Congress Control Number: 2008940732
ISBN-13: 978-1-59863-897-4
ISBN-10: 1-59863-897-1

Course Technology, a part of Cengage Learning
20 Channel Center Street
Boston, MA 02210
USA

Cengage Learning is a leading provider of customized learning solutions with office locations around the globe, including Singapore, the United Kingdom, Australia, Mexico, Brazil, and Japan. Locate your local office at: **international.cengage.com/region**

Cengage Learning products are represented in Canada by Nelson Education, Ltd.

For your lifelong learning solutions, visit **courseptr.com**
Visit our corporate website at **cengage.com**

To the newest member of our family, my nephew Tyler.
Hopefully crazy, psychic Aunt Tiffany won't freak you out too much.

From Psychic/Medium Chip Coffey...

WHAT BETTER PLACE THAN the historic and haunted Stanley Hotel in Estes Park, Colorado, could there be for a first-time meeting between two people who talk to the dead?

I met Tiffany Johnson on our first morning at the Stanley. We were both there to provide readings to the attendees of a paranormal conference. I had ventured into the lobby, hungry for breakfast, and suddenly, down the grand staircase, came this lovely blonde woman whose entrance caused every head in the room to turn in her direction.

Was it my imagination or did the sunlight streaming through the windows behind her further illuminate her already radiant aura? Did I really hear the theme music from *Gone with the Wind* as she descended the stairs?

Within minutes after saying our initial "hellos," Tiff and I were in my rental car, heading down into the village for breakfast together. And the rest is history!

I've traveled all across the country with Tiffany. We've shared hotel rooms, given gallery readings together, laughed and cried and kvetched together. Ours is a priceless friendship.

As a psychic and medium, Tiffany is able to tap into those unexplainable repositories of information that often astound her clients. (And me!)

Do not let her blonde beauty sway you into believing that she's anything but a font of knowledge regarding metaphysical and spiritual subjects. I am frequently blown away by just how much she knows and how eloquently she shares what she knows.

To say that I adore Tiffany is a huge understatement! From day one, she has referred to me as "Doodle," a nickname that somehow came to her and stuck. I hope and pray that she will always be a part of my life, that the love and laughter we share will enrich my life until the day when she'll have to use her skills as a medium to communicate with me.

Even then, I intend to remain her ever-adoring "Doodle."

I know you will enjoy reading Tiffany's book. How do I know this? Hey, I'm a psychic! I know these things!

Acknowledgments

MY WHOLE HOPE in writing this book is to give you, the reader, the good, the better, and the not so great about psychism. Your undertaking, in just trying to *understand* psychic development is noble and honorable. However, there are definitely tough parts to it. Because of this, I want to show all sides and have you really understand who and what came before both you and I.

I'm so grateful to my husband Bobby for constantly believing in my pursuits and me. Without him, I couldn't have fulfilled my dreams and have such great joy in doing what I love professionally. There were many, many times where he was there to bring me down to Earth and to boost me up to my greatest potential. And somehow, he seems to know what to do when.

A huge thank you goes to my mother, Karen, for always giving me the voice to speak my truth. As whacky as that truth may have sounded, she always believed in me. My mom was always there to listen to my new thoughts and feelings about my personal spirituality. With courage and conviction in her parenting, she was the perfect mom for a young, budding psychic. To this day she is my biggest fan. Love you, Mom.

Thank you to all of you who helped me along my way. The path has been long, but so rewarding. Just to mention a few: Becky Wendorff, for giving me my first shot out of the gates. Echo Bodine, for allowing me to work with her and her students. Jeff Belanger, for helping me with this book and keeping me on my toes. Dave Schrader, for bringing me on his events all around the country. Jason Hawes and Grant Wilson, for your constant support and friendship. Kevin Pugh, for putting me on my very first radio station. Chip Coffey, for EVERYTHING. You are my dear friend and have enriched my life more than you'll ever know. Dana Dynamite, for making me look so fantastic. Amber Davies, for assisting me each and every day. Matt Moniz, for your generous knowledge on so many topics. The list could go on and on. I'm certain I have forgotten many here, but you are in my heart forever.

About the Author

TIFFANY JOHNSON is a world-renowned psychic, writer, healer (Reiki Master), media personality, ordained minister, teacher, and speaker. With 20+ years of experience in the psychic realm, there isn't much that Tiffany hasn't encountered. At a young age, Tiffany began her studies with the Tarot and continued to pursue her interests in mediumship, Magick, hypnosis, and various other topics. Now, in her 30s, Tiffany has had the opportunity to work and study with many experts in the spiritual and paranormal field.

Practicing out of Minnesota, but lecturing and providing readings nationally, many find her down-to-earth sense of humor along with her metaphysical knowledge just what they have been looking for on their spiritual journey. She continues to receive regional and national accolades and media attention with her no-nonsense approach, including an appearance on A&E's successful television program, *Psychic Kids*.

In addition to *Picture Yourself Developing Your Psychic Abilities*, Tiffany is the author of *Seeds of Thought* (published in 2004) and is a monthly columnist for www.ghostvillage.com.

Table of Contents

It's a Wild Ride

I ALWAYS SMILE WHEN MY clients start out their session with "This is going to sound crazy, but…" At that point I quickly remind them to whom they are talking. Remember, I'm a PSYCHIC. I've been fortunate enough to have heard it all. Or at least a good portion of it "all." But that doesn't mean that people don't surprise me on a daily basis. They do. Just ask my mom. I tell her that all the time. It's not only the tough stuff, but it's the strength and courage from people that astounds me. It really reignites my faith in Spirit. Hopefully, on your journey of opening up your own psychic abilities, you'll have that same experience.

Some of my favorite work to do (as a psychic and medium) is to provide people with the understanding that there *is* another side that we can't see with physical eyes. There is nothing better in this world than to show parents of a lost (passed over) child that his/her soul lives on and most importantly continues to *love* them. Many times, those sessions end with everyone involved in tears, including me. As painful as the work may be, it's by far the most rewarding I've ever had.

Working and developing your psychic abilities isn't just a part-time hobby. At least it isn't something to take lightly. No matter where you are on your psychic journey, this book will help to give you clarity. Remember: Everyone is psychic. So, even if you consider yourself a beginner, you are on your psychic path. Now it's just becoming more of a focus for you. Considering the vast amount of information out there, you could take up several lifetimes studying all the different avenues and variances in psychic development. But, maybe you have! Maybe this is a continuation of a soul's journey for you. Maybe this is a piece of the theological puzzle you have been working through in this lifetime. Either way, there isn't a lack of material for you to work and study with. Fortunately, there has been research, study, and theory on the idea of psychics and psychism since the dawn of time. In fact, I dare to say that being a psychic was the first profession! Not what we currently believe it to be!

This book is meant to be a history lesson and to set expectations, and be a reference tool and a general guidebook for you on your psychic journey. Hopefully, you can find something that resonates with you in every chapter. Even if you don't agree with the idea or concept, ideally you can retain the knowledge. That's the key point when studying something such as psychic development. There isn't a right answer for all things at all times. Your perceptions will be ever-changing. That's the greatest thing about this path.

In addition to this book, you'll find a DVD video to help you along. I'll show you how to smudge a room and yourself for psychic protection. Further, I'll walk you through a Tarot reading, showing you some tips and tricks when working with that divination tool. My friend, Liz, allowed the cameras to roll as I gave her a reading. In this segment of the video, you will be able to understand how things happen and what can occur during a reading. Lastly, I address several questions that come up not only around psychic development, but also psychic abilities. Throughout this section, you can not only prepare yourself for questions you may receive, but also consider your thoughts around the specific topics addressed.

©istockphoto.com/Daniel Brunner

Think About It

Why Work on Your Psychic Skills?

Why *would* you want to work on your psychic skills? What do you have to gain? Are you looking for ways to assist your friends on their path? Do you want to understand your partner's love? Gain insight into the workings of the universe? Many days, it's all of the above. It's inherently unique to every individual.

I was born with an above average psychic skill set. I had no choice in the matter. I had to deal with my psychic skills at a very young age. You, too, will have to deal with and undertake some things that are not entirely positive.

I remember waking up as a very young child (probably three or four years old) from all the noise and chatter around me. As I lay in bed, I found that perhaps 30 to 40 transparent and shadow-like people surrounded me. As is the case in my adult life, I didn't much care to be woken up at 3:00 AM.

Why Work on Your Psychic Skills?

AFTER A FEW MOMENTS, I would start to listen to the "people." These people would pass along information mainly about my family, although not speaking directly to me. It was more that they were chatting with themselves and I would overhear the conversation. The next morning when mentioning the conversations to my mother, I realized that what these "people" were talking about was past history of my ancestors. Thank God for my mom; she didn't completely freak out. She just asked questions, but didn't push. Honestly, she was my biggest supporter.

©istockphoto.com/Karl Dolenc

From there, I had a very natural inclination to the New Age and all things metaphysical. I started studying Tarot. I looked into healing: astrology, numerology, runes, and angels all held my interest, and still do, even to this day. I went through junior high, high school, and even into college studying and doing readings for friends and family. I want you to know I was very fortunate. I wasn't looked at as a freak, but I did stand out of the crowd. Readings were just something that I did—that was unique to me being Tiffany.

I gave up my corporate career several years ago. I truly believe in my heart of hearts that this was my career destiny. I *needed* to be a professional psychic. But, remember, this is my profession. Most of you, I believe, are just simply looking to expand the psychic within. However, don't rule anything out. This may become your passion as well, and ultimately, your career.

Having that desire, to expand your psychic abilities, will sometimes put you in a precarious position. You'll not only have to recognize and perhaps adjust your belief system, you may, actually, have to explain it to others! And that, my friends, can cause some controversy. Unfortunately, psychism and the many topics around it often make people feel ill at ease.

©istockphoto.com/bobbieo

Okay, that's the bad stuff. But, these are all things that you have to consider. Now, let's talk about the good stuff!

Working on your psychic abilities empowers you, makes you accountable, and probably most importantly, deepens your connection with the divine. Whatever the divine is to you. You'll have the opportunity to give insight, heal, and share your faith with others. What greater gift could there be?

Many people conjure up the idea of psychics as witches. Yes, folks, that belief still runs true today. As crazy as that may sound, psychics, for some people, equal fear. Remember that we are not that far in our history from the "burning times." In the grand scheme of things, that part of our history was just moments ago.

For those who aren't familiar with the term, the "burning times" were a time of persecution by Christians of those who were thought to be non-Christian. Most often, in truth, those who were burned (hence the term "burning times") or hung were Christian but kept to themselves (oftentimes healers and midwives) and were falsely accused of witchcraft. Although these acts mainly occurred from 1550 to 1650, there are historical records of these atrocities happening from the 14th through the 18th centuries in countries including the United States, England, France, and Russia.

©istockphoto.com/knape

Even if you never, ever tell anyone or mention your interest or your study, you can use these techniques to assist others in a passive way. Remember, you are under NO obligation to share with anyone what you "pick up." All psychic information is up to you to do with what you wish. Naturally, I believe that we all, at our core, want to help those that we love and care about. With your new skills, you'll be able to do just that. And with it, really discover more about you and your soul.

Ultimately, this is why we all want to discover the psychic inside each of us: To deepen our knowledge about ourselves. It's only through deep understanding of why we are the way we are that we hope to evolve into broader and deeper human beings. And then, through our evolution, we can assist those on their personal journeys in this lifetime. Hopefully, within the pages of this book, through the instruction within, you'll accomplish your psychic goals.

©istockphoto.com/Florea Marius

What Is a Psychic?

MAYBE IT'S EASIER TO SPEAK to what a psychic isn't. Often, when we eliminate certain things and thoughts, we can better define the truth around a subject. So, let's start there.

A psychic is not a mind reader. I think that is the most common perception, or, better said, mis-perception. Often, when I tell people what I do for a living, many people respond with "get out of my head." Or, conversely, they ask me what they are thinking at the time. I can't read minds, nor would I choose to if I had the choice. Reading a mind isn't really gaining information, it's just transmitting it. Projecting it, if you will.

©istockphoto.com/Andrew Howe

A psychic is not a "fixer upper." Unfortunately, psychics are not repair persons, bankers, investors, or firemen. We can only pass along the information that we receive. Fortunately (and it may seem unfortunate at times), our clients are the only ones who can dictate what happens in their own lives. There are no magic formulas for anyone. All we do is give insight.

Everyone is fortunate to have "free will." What I mean by this is anyone can do exactly what he or she wants to do at any given time. No one is a robot. We all make our own choices and really, it's a blessing that we can make those choices. The upset is when we make poor decisions and react to other people's issues. The bottom line is nothing, and no one, can be controlled.

Another way of thinking about free will is this: I could drive from Minneapolis to Dallas via Los Angeles. Is this the best way? It may be. Is it the *quickest,* most efficient route? Probably not. However, it might be the right path *for me.* That, in essence, is free will. We pick and choose on a moment-to-moment, hour-to-hour, day-to-day basis what feels right and works best with every opportunity. We'll talk more about free will later in the chapter.

A psychic is not a counselor. It's a very rare occurrence that a psychic has a PhD, M.D., or any other medical diploma/certification. Albeit that we, as psychics, hear all sorts of family issues, relationship issues, financial issues, professional issues, and so on, most would never claim to give you a solution on how to resolve a particular problem. Again, the role of the psychic is to give you information. That information is to be used in a way for you to make better decisions in your own life.

It's unfortunate, but some psychics are looking to take away an individual's own accountability or control in their own lives. Hasn't everybody heard of the psychic that will remove the "family curse"? They'll be happy to burn candles and say prayers for a couple weeks for a substantial fee. This, I'm afraid to tell you, is not a real psychic. They may have gifts and abilities; however, the lack of ethics and integrity take away any substance that they may have.

A psychic is not a punching bag. I think that statement says it all. I, again, can only give you information around your life, about your life, and what may be in your best interest. What you do with that information is 100% up to you, as the receiver of that information. What the receiver chooses to do with his life cannot be blamed or credited to psychics. It's a wonderful thing, as a psychic, to be validated and thanked. However, it's not necessary. In the same token, faulting or accusing a psychic of your own indiscretion is never fair or warranted. You are the boss of you.

A psychic is not a gossip "monger." I realize that we all are concerned about our family, friends, and loved ones. I get it. However, a psychic is not going to tell you if your neighbor is having an affair on his spouse. It has no bearing on your life. You will not live and die by that information. In the same token, asking about a coworker and her purported plastic surgery will not make or break your career. This is not the type of information a psychic should pass along. Now, asking about your mother's well being is completely understood and okay. Wanting to know the outlook of your son's future is well and good. Hopefully, you see the major difference in these inquiries. In upcoming chapters, we'll work on techniques and tools you can use to gain this information for yourself.

There are some major ethical, moral, and integrity issues that surround psychics. In the past, there have been some subpar people in the psychic industry who, unfortunately, have given psychics/intuitives/sensitives (amateur and professional) a fairly bad reputation. (I don't think I need to name names here. We'll talk more about the public's perceptions on psychics later in this chapter.) It's unfortunate, but some nationally known psychics have been caught in lies, extorting money, and so forth. Whether or not you want to do this to broaden your own life or are considering it as a profession, how you conduct yourself impacts all psychics.

Some ethical issues you may need to consider are (other than the gossip issues above): charging for your readings, confidentiality, honesty, frequency of readings, and peer review.

Most of the things go hand-in-hand. Charging unreasonable amounts for your readings (if you choose to charge at all) is pretty straightforward. Beyond that, confidentiality and honesty are paramount. As a psychic, you need to always be honest with yourself and completely honest with your clientele. You must have due diligence to those you read for at all times. Which may include "cutting off" someone who repeatedly comes to you for readings. Unfortunately, some people begin to rely too heavily on the information that you receive as a psychic. At that point, it's your job to re-empower your client. Lastly, it may come to your attention that someone else doing readings is misleading people. *You* have to make a decision how you want to handle that. Personally, I decided long ago that I would never dispute or put down another reader publicly. But, that's my choice.

So what *is* a psychic? I believe a psychic is a tool. That's it. I don't mean that in a degrading way. Any psychic simply is a conduit of messages from the universe. We are simply opening up and allowing ourselves the opportunity to hear subtle information given off by Spirit/God/universe. It's very much like having a natural aptitude towards anything else. Some may see the subtle beauty in a painting or piece of art. We, as psychics, receive the subtle vibrations around us. As such, we are able to pass those messages onto those around us. That is our duty. Ultimately, we are a translator for what the divine wants to pass along.

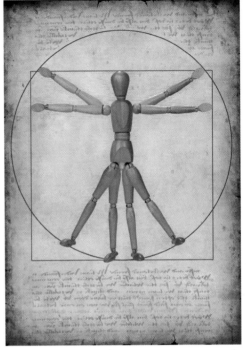

©istockphoto.com/Gino Santa Maria

One last thing about what a psychic is: Human. In no way do we have leverage, power, or anything else over anybody else. As our psychic abilities develop and open up, we need to understand and be grateful for the connection. In no way should we ever take advantage of our gift. Understand that through our development, we *will* make mistakes. But, that's what makes us better. Better at "tuning in" and better people as a whole. Remember, psychics put their pants on one leg at a time just like everybody else. We, as psychics, are mothers, business people, brothers, and friends. Same as anybody else.

The Public's Perception of Psychics

I'T'S NO SECRET that the public perception of a psychic is a little… out there. Part of that lies in the historical aspects of psychics. But we'll talk more about the history later. Some of the ideas come from Hollywood. Others from psychics themselves. All in all, it's a varied perception to say the least. Fortunately, the thoughts and perceptions around psychics and what they do are currently changing in the public's eye.

©istockphoto.com/pidjoe

There are a few general, stereotypical psychic "types" or portrayals of psychics out there. Now, these often are professionals (and I use that term somewhat loosely) in the public eye doing readings for the general population. Unfortunately, some of these ideas are not necessarily positive. And, typically, they are not a very accurate portrayal. Let's look at a few representations:

First, let's talk about what I like to call the "woo woo la la" psychic. This is the person who will only speak to energy. He or she may be very focused on spirit (which is a wonderful thing, but they often need grounding), love, and the angels. They often speak in very vague terms, rarely giving tangible, practical information. Using esoteric language, they discuss the "vibe" around you and possibly karmic issues. They are wonderful at making you feel good about you, but rarely have any tangible substance to what they provide. Remember, the exercises that are provided in upcoming chapters will help you gain *specific* information for your querent to work with.

©istockphoto.com/Eva Serrabassa

They may focus on what is hindering you and by all means, that may be beneficial. However, they may get stuck there, in the negative aspects of day-to-day life. Unfortunately, any psychic that points out the struggles in life and does not focus on what can be done to fix them is pointless.

Another is the "kitchen" psychic. This psychic could be your neighbor, child's teacher, grocer, or your dental hygienist. They don't have a look or attitude to go along with anyone. They are what can be termed as quite normal. They sit at their kitchen tables or in their living rooms working on their psychic abilities, giving readings to friends and family in a very casual way. Honestly, I think most psychics are exactly this. Generally low key, ordinary people looking within themselves to connect however they can. The down side to these psychics is that sometimes they don't have the confidence to share their gifts with those who would really appreciate and respect it.

Now, here is a fun one. The "gypsy" psychic. These people often claim heritage from a Mediterranean area. In addition, they "feed" the stereotypical look of a psychic. Often wearing bohemian type clothing, utilizing dark rooms, and, perhaps, even feigning a slight, nondescript accent. Mostly in very urban settings, utilizing flashing neon signs to advertise, these psychics give low-cost, initial readings to the public. However, they are usually the ones that mention the family curse, dark entity, etc. that needs to be immediately "removed." And they're happy to take care of this for you for the low, low price of $2,000. I have heard time and time again that these people are often very accurate with their initial consultation, but unfortunately, fall short in the ethics department.

This next one often has a bit of a fear element to him or her. They are what I like to call the "witch" or "gothic" psychic. This is not to put down my Pagan/Wiccan friends out there. (I can't stress that enough.) I respect, honor, and admire that belief system and often find myself connecting with it. This brand of psychic may wear a lot of black, seems quite ominous (almost vampiric looking), and may, just by the physical presence, make you feel a little uneasy.

Fortune teller broach.

9

As you can see, psychics, just like any other group in society, are varied. All have their own flaws. Of course, I'm only using random generalizations, but I want you to know right up front what label may be put on *you* when you come out of the "psychic" closet! I understand it's not fair that we have *any* sort of stereotypes (i.e., blondes being dumb; lawyers being greedy), but it's the way we, as human beings, are built. This book is meant to prepare you in EVERY way to be a psychic, not just working on technique. So, as such, we have to examine and ultimately, realize the vast concept of being psychic.

On an exciting note, at this very time, right now, perceptions are changing! For the first time ever, psychics are, in a very general way, understood. Even though the stigmas of the past still somewhat permeate society, at the very *least,* people know what a psychic is! A lot of this has to be credited to the media in all forms. Television has highly successful shows featuring psychics on major networks. With various reality-based paranormal shows, sitcoms, and dramas featuring mediums and psychics, the general public is becoming more educated. (Although many are works of fiction, I'll take it!) Radio stations frequently have guests on speaking toward psychic development, the paranormal, and spirituality! In fact, many have a "regular repeat" psychic that listeners can call in to on a weekly or monthly basis. Movies are being made on the concept of precognition. Colleges are teaching courses in intuition. You can see how concepts and thoughts are really transforming!

Tiffany in front of a typical psychic shop in Manhattan.

To what degree you put yourself out to the community as a psychic will depend on your comfort level. You may want to keep your interest and studies to yourself, and that's perfectly okay! You may want to reach out and take some courses at a local metaphysical store or Unity church. Having a support group is wonderful and can be so beneficial not only to your psychic development, but also to the emotional transition of delving deeper into your spiritual side. Or, you may want to take this to an even higher level. It may be your calling to be a psychic by profession. That choice takes a lot of hard work, thick skin, and discipline. Whatever you decide, know that it's right for you right now. You may delve further into your studies and make a different decision later. Nothing is fixed.

Reaching Out to What Can't Be Seen

UNFORTUNATELY, THERE is a lack of hard science to back up psychic ability. The bottom line is that psychic ability has no tangible evidence. We can't see how it works. There have been countless "soft" studies by psychologists, colleges, and universities, and numerous "outside," seemingly indifferent, groups (including the U.S. government). Everyone wants to understand and recognize what, really, can't be explained. Although a psychic can communicate how he or she receives information through whatever means, it's very difficult to prove. What we can validate is, ultimately, the information that is received through the psychic.

The "how" is the big question in psychicism. For as many different types of psychics, there are just as many ways of receiving information. Not only that, but we all interpret the information in ways that are unique to us. Think about it this way: When you hear something from a friend about anything at all, you immediately relate it to your past experiences, your education, and what you know about the individual. As a psychic, you'll do the same thing. Because this is the case, there are infinite ways of passing along psychic material. So, we run back into the question(s) of how we receive the information. I do believe that someday this question will be answered, but for the time being, we'll just have to be patient.

Not answering the "how" question, but at least giving us the knowledge that there is *something* tangible going on with psychic abilities is the aspect of proven accuracy. Sure, there are a lot of charlatans out there that try to give psychics a bad name, but they are quickly weeded out due to the one major factor that moral psychics have—and, again, that's accuracy. Thank goodness accuracy really regulates the psychic. We don't have much else to cling to. Accuracy in readings can be proven. Period. Now, it may not be proven immediately, but it can be proven. In a reading, information may come up that is not immediately validated by the querent. However, the reasons for this may be many. The person may not know a historical fact that is being brought in by the psychic. Another reason may be that the psychic is picking up on a future event. Another still may be an issue going on with someone else other than the person getting the reading. Until the querent communicates with the person the reading may be in reference to, it cannot be proven. You get the drift.

My Story

I've had a number of wonderful experiences of clients coming to me with feedback and validation of accuracy. One of my favorite stories is when three women came to see me one afternoon. All three had never had prior readings, and really didn't know what to expect. Because of this, the reading was open to whatever came through. As I sat with the eldest of the three women (she was the mother AND mother-in-law to the other two gals), she sat in front of me, arms crossed, scowling. She began the session telling me that she didn't know why she was wasting her money and her very valuable time. However, she wanted to have some special time with her family, so she "gave in" to this reading. Needless to say, this wasn't the best opening of a reading I had ever had. However, saying a little prayer internally, I began the reading. Over and over I received information of her health being in jeopardy. I heard coughing. I saw a thermometer showing me a fever. I saw cloudy lungs. Now, as I'm not a doctor, I didn't diagnose the symptoms, just conveyed to her what I was receiving. She, very *abruptly* told me that she didn't know what I was talking about. She didn't smoke. She felt fine and she was in perfect health. Unfortunately, this was how the entire reading went.

At this point in time in my career, I recorded all my clients' readings for them as a memento. Something that would benefit me in this instance. After our session, she, again, told me how this was a waste and one of the other women came in for her reading. It was two weeks later that I received a call from one of the other women that came to see me. Upon their travels home, they listened to one another's tape recordings. They each heard the other's reading. The woman that called me wanted me to know that approximately four hours *after* the reading, the woman that complained about her reading the entire time had been suddenly taken to the emergency room due to a severe case of pneumonia.

Accuracy, being the one true test of a psychic, still has one issue: free will. We spoke a bit about it earlier. Free will is our God-given choice to do what we want at any given time. Individuals have free will. Family units have free will. Corporations have free will and so on and so forth. That being the case, a psychic may pick up on or have a "hit" on a certain topic that is coming through as part of an upcoming event.

©istockphoto.com/Alex Slobodkin

Letting the querent know about the upcoming situation may change the ultimate outcome, therefore adjusting the accuracy. I say "adjusting" for a very specific reason. It's not that the psychic didn't come through with correct information; the person receiving the reading had an opportunity to change, hopefully for the best, the outcome. Let's look at it another way. Say someone came to me and asked if they were going to lose weight and the best way to do so. I could speak to a diet or perhaps an exercise regimen. IF that person chose, after the reading, to go out and eat a quart of ice cream, that would be his choice. His free will would allow him to make that decision. Would I have been inaccurate in what came through? Maybe. However, due to the change in path that the client made, we'll never know.

I want to take a minute to talk about the psychic that claims to be 100% accurate. Now, having had the discussion about accuracy, you can see for yourself that this simply could never be true. NO psychic is 100% right on all the time. In fact, when studies are done, psychic ability is considered to be anything over 60% accurate. Beyond that, think about this: Has the psychic making that claim followed up with every person that he has done a reading on, reviewing every topic that was mentioned in the reading itself? Probably not. Heck, that would be a task that wouldn't leave time for anything else!

When you reach out psychically, there often is the question about tuning in to something negative. Call it what you will. Demon. Negative consciousness. Discarnate entity. Whatever. There's a lot of concern around it. Here's the thing: You, most likely, will *feel* if something isn't right or positive. It's our biological make up that can often discern what isn't from the light. You'll get nauseous. You may feel light-headed or dizzy.

You'll know. The issue comes forth, however, when you don't pay attention to those feelings. Please know that doesn't happen often. I can't stress enough that this is not the norm. Do you need to be aware of it? Of course. Is it something that you should have a consciousness about? Sure. But realize that it is nothing that you should be fearful of. Your focused intention is what will keep you safe.

Lastly, remember that everything has psychic energy. It's imprinted on to every*thing* as much as every*body.* The chair that you sit in will have residual psychic imprints. Your favorite hat will hold past energies. Heck, even this book will! As you learn to develop your psychic abilities, you'll realize that this skill, too, will help you get clarification on what you're interpreting. In the same notion, realize that it is not a current "broadcast" (so to speak) but one left after an issue(s). The ability to read items is called *psychometry*, but we'll talk more about that later in another chapter.

©istockphoto.com/Dawn Poland

©istockphoto.com/Mariya Bibikova

Psychics in Society

HISTORY HAS REVERED AND RECORDED many psychics (often called "prophets," as the word "psychic" didn't gain popularity until the late 1850s); so many, I could never cover all of them. Unfortunately, as much as we know about psychics and the abilities therein, we don't have a positive perception looking back in time.

History

L ET'S LOOK INTO THE BACKGROUND and reputations of a few of the more famous psychics. From them, we can better understand the basis of the current societal views. From there, we can hope to gain the same specific insights that they received for our forefathers.

Witch of Endor

The story regarding the Witch of Endor comes to us through the biblical story of King Saul in the first book of Samuel. This "witch" was a woman who had a talisman that purportedly allowed her some mediumship (speaking to those who have passed over) abilities. Much like psychics of today, King Saul sought her out to gain insight and information on the outcome against the Philistines. Unfortunately, the reading that he received wasn't positive. She foretold (utilizing the spirit or "ghost" of Samuel) his downfall as king. The next day, Saul and his sons died in battle.

SAUL AND THE WITCH OF ENDOR.

©istockphoto.com/Duncan Walker

Unfortunately, this is only one of the beginnings in the subpar reputation of psychics. As we all know, it's often the messenger that gets "shot." In this story, the issue begins where Saul seeks out the "witch" at the onset. God, prior to his meeting with the medium, supposedly spoke to Saul and told him not to seek out other sources for information. So, strike one. Then he gets the news that he will fall as the King of Israel.

Strike two. To top it off, after finding out this information, he dies, as do members of his family. Not a great outcome. As we know, history is written by the "winners," or at least the survivors. As such, when this tale was passed along, the negative focus was put on the "witch" as she seemingly was the pivot point where things turned bad.

Oracle at Delphi

Another historic psychic was the Oracle at Delphi. The priestess, who was chosen upon the death of her predecessor, was a woman of good standing in the community (sometimes wealthy, other times a peasant) and often held great power. She would sit over an open cavern in the earth and prophesize about the future affairs of the community, government, and sometimes personal situations. It has been speculated that the visions given to these women (there were many oracles over the course of several hundred years) were due to gasses (either methane or ethylene) in the cavern that would seep up into the temple causing them to hallucinate. Oftentimes, their visions had to be interpreted as it was said that the women were "overtaken" in spirit. This temple, linked to Apollo, existed until approximately 395 A.D.

Here, the idea of vague messages becomes an issue. At one point in history, this was seen as the "norm"—that those who received visions would have those around them that would and could interpret the communication. This happened for two reasons. One, there was a strong reigning class in society. Those who interpreted were typically educated and considered superior and could relate the psychic information to the other classes. The second reason was the interpretations could be molded to whatever situation was at hand and conformed to what would be most pleasing to those in charge. Here, in the present, psychics are constantly fighting those skeptics who say that their messages could apply to various issues around anyone.

©istockphoto.com/Dennis Guyitt

Nostradamus

Nostradamus was a famous seer and psychic. He's most famous for the quatrains (four-lined poems) that prophesized worldly occurrences (notably the French Revolution and the atomic bomb, to mention only a couple). His professional career began as an apothecary, but after the death of his wife and children, he turned more to the occult. His book, *Les Prophetcies* (published in 1555), became very popular, spreading his visions to the public. Even to this day, his works are still very popular. However, they are written in such a way that it is very difficult to understand the meaning of them prior to an event occurring. Hence, they do little to predict the future.

©istockphoto.com/HuttonArchive

Here again, we are faced with the nature of the psychic information fitting only *after* an event happens, making the communication look somewhat contrived or, perhaps, melded into what we want to fit. Due to the circular speak of his quatrains, only Nostradamus himself would know, fully, if what he predicted came to pass. Or, if we, so eager to validate his divine connection, are putting things together that shouldn't be.

It's easy to see where a potential fear of psychics comes from. It permeates our history. Even in these few, brief examples, you can see that society is not only conditioned to potentially fear psychics (they may predict your death!), but to also chastise them as going "against God" (Leviticus 20:27: "A man or woman who is a medium or spiritist among you must be put to death. You are to stone them; their blood will be on their own heads.") or condemn them as frauds (they only tell you what you want to hear!). It's not a great reputation, but it's one that is changing. Thank goodness that with time, feelings and thoughts dilute, and rationalization, understanding, tolerance, and education permeate.

The European and American witch trials or "burning times" are horrific examples of psychics being feared in their communities. During these times (approximately between the 1500s and 1700s), people feared anyone who perhaps had otherworldly skills. Those who had knowledge of healing, herbalism, animal communication, and certainly psychic abilities were quickly accused. At a minimum they were discriminated against, and in the worst case, put to death. Due to the strict, fundamental religious nature of the puritanical peoples, this seemed lawful and just.

Unfortunately, the Bible has various verses that are interpreted to be against psychics and psychism. I mentioned the Leviticus verse above. Here are others:

▶ **Deuteronomy 18:10-12: "Let no one be found among you who sacrifices his son or daughter in the fire, who practices divination or sorcery, interprets omens, engages in witchcraft, or casts spells or who is a medium or spiritist or who consults the dead."**

▶ **Isaiah 8:19: "When they say to you 'Consult the mediums and spiritist who whisper and mutter,' should not all people consult their God? Should they consult the dead on behalf of the living?"**

Like all things, you can read quite a bit into each of these verses. Overall, the Bible warns against "false" prophets. Again, there are many verses that speak to this issue. The bottom line is this: God (Spirit) wants no one to be misled or to have anyone taken advantage of. In addition, no one should solely rely upon another for insight. Ultimately the truth, in any matter, needs to be between you and your own faith. As such, let's remember this verse as well for balance:

1 Corinthians 12:10: To another the working of miracles; to another prophecy; to another discerning of spirits; to another diverse kinds of tongues; to another the interpretation of tongues.

Famous Psychics

JUST LIKE EVERYTHING ELSE, we can't understand and develop any skill set unless we understand who and what came before our interest in the matter. As such, we need to explore not only the history, but also those who broke ground for us in more present time.

Before we explore any of our forefathers/mothers, we need to conclude ONE very important thing. Fame and celebrity do not mean accuracy, integrity, or perfection. Those I'll mention did something very important: They broke ground for us as psychics and brought it to the community on a larger level. In and of itself, that's a very important accomplishment. Definitely something to respect and admire. It's only in more recent times that individuals could have mass appeal, as the technology, in our history, wasn't there.

The Fox Sisters

The Fox Sisters were three sisters (Margaret, Kate, and Leah) from New York who all, from a very young age, showed a great deal of psychic abilities. These ladies were, ultimately, the founders and leaders of the Spiritualist movement (which is still alive and well to this day). As young girls, Kate and Margaret experienced "rapping" (as they called it). This "rapping" allowed the girls to communicate with a spirit that was allegedly in their family home. As the news of their communications grew, so did their reputations. To try to subdue the news, the girls were split up. Kate went to live with her sister,

Leah, and Margaret went to live with her brother, David. However, the "rapping" continued, as did their notoriety. Both Kate and Margaret became quite famous in New York for providing public séances where they attracted quite a bit of attention from other notable people in the community. Ultimately, Kate and Margaret both developed quite severe drinking problems and Leah fell out of favor with both.

From this story, we see where fame can overtake not only your own life, but also that of your families'. Not unlike show business, the idea of an audience and attention became so attractive it ultimately destroyed the family. Later in life, hoping to gain a little more exposure, Margaret, herself, came out and confessed what she claimed to be the truth: That the "rappings" were fraudulent. However, since she didn't get the attention she was looking for, she rescinded the confession a year after giving it.

Madam Blavatsky

Madam Blavatsky (otherwise known as Helena Blavatsky) was the founder of the Theosophical Society and was known for her great psychic abilities. Known for her feats of levitation, telepathy, mediumship, and, most notably, materialization (making items appear out of thin air), she wrote several books that she professed to give insight into the secrets of man (woman). Often the subject of controversy, she was continually being pursued by skeptics who were looking to prove her a fake (and in some instances investigators did get confessions from those who purportedly assisted her in demonstrations). Regardless of her realism, Madam Blavatsky was one of the foremost (if not *the* leader) leaders of the New Age movement.

Once again we run into the aspect of the psychic not meeting snuff. It's unfortunate, but *despite* the psychic gifts that she may have had (and probably was quite adept), she felt the need to overcompensate and provide more of a show than to just relay psychic information. It's unfortunate that due to her celebrity, she and/or her handlers felt the need to create falsehoods.

21

Edgar Cayce

Edgar Cayce could be perceived as the greatest American prophet. Born in Hopkinsville, Kentucky, Mr. Cayce was born into a poor farming family and had a grand total of a ninth-grade education. Known as the "sleeping prophet," he provided readings from a trance-like state on everything from health issues to reincarnation to business advice. When brought out of the trance, he claimed he was unable to recall any information given to the person requesting the information. Over the course of his life, he gave 13,000 to 14,000 readings. What was quite remarkable, and ultimately unexplainable, was that Mr. Cayce, while in the trance, often spoke about things that he had no prior knowledge of (nor had the education to account for, remembering that he only entered the ninth grade), including the biology of the body and geographic phenomena. In 1931, Mr. Cayce started the Association for Research and Enlightenment (A.R.E.) and the organization is still going strong today.

Edgar Cayce (used with permission from A.R.E.)

We are fortunate that with Edgar Cayce, there were very few skeptics lurking to diminish his reputation. Albeit that criticism has been around the study of portions of his readings, very few have come right out against Mr. Cayce, truly making him one of the most influential, highly respected leaders in the psychic community. This man of deep conviction and love of Spirit broke ground not only in the realm of psychic perceptions, but he also contributed greatly to the entire awareness of consciousness.

As you have probably deduced, developing your psychic abilities isn't and can't be about the potential fame. Ego cannot play a role when looking within and working with others. It's a wonderful thing to be validated and have confirmation on what you receive (and I promise you will!), but that isn't what this path is about. It's about evolving the soul, and hopefully, if you're lucky, being able to share with others insights and inspiration.

Psychics in the Media

WITH THE ONSET OF NEW and numerous technologies, we've all had the opportunity to see psychics at work. Love 'em or hate 'em, it's pretty nifty to be able to watch how they connect. Not only that, but we get to experience, along with an audience, the effect that a psychic can have on an individual. Also, we have the ability to contact and schedule a reading with various psychics around the world. From 900 numbers to call-in television shows to internet chats, psychics are in the media.

There is a lot of controversy about what is created and portrayed by Hollywood. With the creation of reality shows, psychics on talk shows, paranormal shows, science-fiction programs, and dramatic portrayals, there are many thoughts about what a psychic is and is not. Let me say this outright, as thoughtful as some shows may be to provide an accurate representation (speaking especially to reality-based programming), there is always the aspect of entertainment. Shows are edited down to approximately five percent (at most) of what is really filmed. A typical one-hour program will often film for five days. Only a *fraction* of the total event is distributed. No one is to blame for this situation. The cast is paid to do their job(s). The production crew is paid to shoot. The production company needs to edit film to make it fit a timeslot. The network then provides the timeslot and sells advertising during that space to make more revenue to pay for more shows. You can see where each aspect has its own agenda.

All things considered, I would rather have an audience partially understand psychicism rather than have no concept of it at all! Let's talk more specifically about "media" psychics. Here are a few examples.

©istockphoto.com/Shaun Lowe

Sylvia Browne

One of the most heavily "exposed," so to speak, psychics is Sylvia Browne. Ms. Browne is not only a well-known psychic, but also a best-selling author of over 30 books. Featured weekly on the Montel Williams show (now since cancelled), she gained even more of an audience and popularity providing short, brief readings for audience members. In addition, she has been featured on the Larry King Show several times, also doing readings for those who call in. There is no question that Ms. Browne may be one of the most visible psychics in the United States, if not in the world. Love her or hate her, Sylvia Browne very much led the way and broke ground for psychics to be understood by society.

Of course, the exposure brings quite a bit of scrutiny. The skeptic, James Randi, and Ms. Browne have had an ongoing feud for years. He claims that she utilizes "hot" and "cold" reading techniques and really has no unique psychic skill. In addition, Ms. Browne's first husband (she has had four husbands), Gary Dufresne (and father of her son and professional psychic, Chris Dufresne), has claimed that her psychic abilities are a hoax. Furthermore, Ms. Browne has been in question about her generalized predictions for years at a time. Unfortunately, she has not been 100% accurate (which is an unrealistic ideal) and those who are out to discredit her, feed on this issue.

John Edward

John Edward is a well-known psychic born in Glen Cove, New York. At a very young age, Mr. Edward received a reading from another psychic claiming that he would, in his adult life, become a very famous psychic, writing books and appearing on television. Apparently, that reading came true. Mr. Edward *has* written several books, produced several audio books, and has had two shows of his own. His first, Crossing Over with John Edward, was prompted by a 1998 appearance on Larry King Live in which callers were so excited to speak with the medium that they overloaded the switchboard. Crossing Over was on various networks; however, it is now off the air. After two years of being away from television, Mr. Edward began another TV project. His new show, aptly named John Edward Cross Country, allows Mr. Edwards the opportunity to travel nationwide (US), speaking to large audiences and providing his readings.

Here again, James Randi (professional skeptic and critic) has made several claims against Mr. Edward. All in all, he makes the same repeated claims that he does of most psychics. That they utilize "cold" and "hot" reading techniques. Another point of controversy that John Edward has run into, in a more general regard, is the aspect of editing his own shows. Some people reported that they sat in a studio for over eight hours to get a one-hour show, claiming that Mr. Edward had "miss after miss" and that the production staff edited away any inconsistency that would take away Mr. Edward's legitimacy. Whatever you believe, John Edward put himself out to the public in a way that many would choose not to. For that, he deserves respect.

Allison Dubois

Allison Dubois is probably best known as the inspiration for the hugely popular hit, Medium (NBC). Ms. Dubois, a native of Arizona (born January 24th, 1972), claims to have had psychic/ medium experiences since she was six years old. Ms. Dubois was subject to a lengthy University of Arizona study performed by tenured professor Dr. Gary Schwartz, who adamantly claims that Alison Dubois has, through evidence proven in the study, psychic abilities. In addition to her work as a psychic, she has authored three books all dealing with the afterlife and the other side. Not caring for the term "psychic," Ms. Dubois prefers to call herself a "profiler" and medium.

Ms. Dubois says that every episode of the hit TV show is not a biography of her life. Rather, it presents situations that she has found herself in with the help of Hollywood glamour. As such, she perceives the show to be an accurate portrayal of her life. In various episodes, her character works primarily with law enforcement agencies. In real life, although Ms. Dubois claims to also have those connections, none have been validated by any credible source.

Everyone Is Psychic

I CAN'T STRESS THIS POINT enough. Everyone, and I mean everyone, is psychic. It's just part of who we are as human beings. No one has an ability that someone else doesn't. That goes for all aspects of learning. Some may have different predispositions to things, but we all have the capacity, and that's something to remember throughout your studies. It's as simple as this: Your brother or sister may have an extraordinary gift for art. And, even though you have the same parents, you may not have the same tendencies. However, you might be tremendously talented in math. You see where people have strengths. This doesn't mean that you can't apply yourself and become a wonderful artist and, conversely, your sibling can certainly acquire the skills in mathematics.

I once knew a wonderful tattoo artist. He was very upfront in telling me that he never formally studied art. That he really just loved the idea of creating something beautiful. So, he applied himself. He was the first person to let you know that his skill set wasn't innately within. He applied himself in every way, everyday to become the success that he was. Because he did this, he explained that he, *not* as a gifted artist, but one who dedicated himself, felt that he could

©istockphoto.com/Cristian Ardelean

appreciate not only his creations but the art itself that much more. So, I say this to you: It doesn't matter where you are on the psychic skill level. It doesn't matter. Because as a trained psychic, rather than a natural one, you may very well tend to appreciate your development that much more. And, very shortly, I'm going to show you how to develop that side of you.

For those of you who may have some stronger predispositions, don't rest on your laurels. We all could study psychicism for the rest of our lives and never come to a real conclusion. There are just so many concepts to learn, it would be hard to master them all. You, as a natural psychic, just have a head start. Often, when people have experiences, it draws them into the exploration of "Why?" And, in studying psychism, spirituality, or metaphysics, when one question gets answered, another one typically appears. In that vein, allow yourself to be flexible when you learn. You may find something that resonates with you initially, but as you continue on your path, it may not feel as "right." That's OK. No one but you decides what works for you and what doesn't.

Another thing to remember as your abilities develop is that they are not "powers." The word "power" used in the connotation of psychic ability implies that you have something over another person. That simply isn't the case. Again, everyone has some psychic aptitude within them. If you start referring to yourself as having special "gifts" (another term I'm not too fond of) it implies that you have some leverage that others don't. So, I highly recommend using the term "abilities" or "tendencies." It may seem to be a small thing. Words are just words, right? Not necessarily. As you start to speak with others about your experiences and what you are pursuing

(if you choose to talk about your studies at all), you need to remember that the topic of psychics already may be taboo. To put people in an uncomfortable place, possibly making them feel as if they are less than you, would not only do you no good, but wouldn't benefit your studies.

Albeit we focused on the notable psychics in time, do not forget that developing your psychic aptitude(s) will not necessarily bring you fame. It may make you unique. It *certainly* may draw attention to you (good and not so good). You may have a special insight into events around you. However, more often than not, there is a long path to walk as a developing psychic. And let me make this clear: It's a wonderful path, but sometimes we all need to take our lumps. Fortunately, the path of a psychic is one, often, of strong faith. And that faith, in whatever you choose, will get you through. Also, that faith, which is ultimately the universal law, will determine and let you know if and when you need to be more in the public eye.

The psychics (whether or not they declared themselves as such) mentioned in this chapter broke much ground not only in the public perceptions, but how we study and take in (psychically) information. They all contributed in a great way. From a historical perspective, we learned that we could impact people greatly for a very long period of time. It's something to remember as we learn to communicate what we receive as psychics. Furthermore, we have to recall that what may be documented (historically or through the media) may not be an exact truth. Lastly, it's most important to not get into psychicism for egotistical reasons. That can readily backfire as we know that certain public perceptions are still maintained by a portion of society looking to discredit psychics.

©istockphoto.com/pidjoe

The "Clairs"

REALLY, WHEN IT COMES DOWN to it, there are only four psychic aptitudes. Many people *use* the word psychic to describe various people who work in divination (foreseeing or foretelling of possible future events), but it's not entirely accurate. Using a tool, such as Tarot or Astrology, isn't a bad thing; it's just not a true psychic ability. The etymology of the word "psychic" is the Greek word *psychikos*, which means of *or* from the soul. Now, if something comes from the soul, it's not utilizing something externally. It's all internal. Seemingly, something from nothing. A modern definition of the word "psychic" is someone who is sensitive to nonphysical forces and influences. Here again, *non*physical. So, since we don't utilize something beyond ourselves that, by definition, creates a psychic situation.

What I want you, as the beginner, to be very clear of is how all the psychic skills *really* work. Not how they are portrayed in the media. So, it may be time to forget what you have seen prior. It's not startling. It's really not scary. In fact, it's very subtle. So subtle that sometimes we fail to notice the nuances in psychic work. As all psychic information flows through us via our Third Eye Chakra, we need to pull apart the different ways it is delivered.

Why Work on Your Psychic Skills?

Clairvoyance IS A FRENCH word meaning, "clear seeing," or "clear sight." Ultimately, it's clairvoyance that gets portrayed most in psychic scenarios. Typically, clairvoyance is not at all like seeing with your physical eyes. More than anything, it's most similar to a situation where you're recalling a memory. Only the memory is not yours. It's given to you from another channel, shown to you, although it's not an occurrence that you have had. Many people who have clairvoyant tendencies liken it to having a movie run through their mind—albeit very quick and sometimes without sound. It's not that you see the movie with your physical eyes, but the inner eye in your mind. Auras, too, are seen clairvoyantly. But we'll talk more about them in Chapter 5.

Clairvoyance is completely different from telepathy. Telepathy, really, is reading someone's mind. They are projecting something to or at you and you receive it. Clairvoyance, again, is receiving information from something beyond the physical. You aren't picking up a thought, want, need, or wish from anyone. Nor is it that you are tuning in to residual energies from something inanimate. That would be considered a form of telepathy.

©istockphoto.com/Duncan Walker

Telepathy is often tested with what is known as the Zener cards. These are five cards with different symbols (circle, plus sign, wavy lines, star, and a square). The tester "sends" the "receiver" the symbol that is shown on the card that is flipped (only to be seen by the tester) and it's noted how often the "receiver" picks the correct symbol. That is a classic study of telepathy, not clairvoyance.

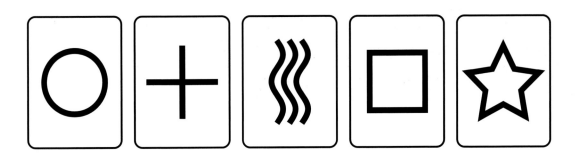

Visions are what clairvoyants receive. Whether it is a series of events (like a mini-movie) or random objects given to the psychic one at a time, since it is visual, it can be called a vision. Visions can be quite literal, or they may be a metaphor. Either way, the observance needs to be noted and communicated if possible. Remember, it is not your job, as a psychic, to interpret the information.

It's your opportunity, and really your only task, to simply pass along the communication. I have found it best not to second-guess what is being shown, as trivial as it may seem to me. So we have due diligence to our recipients to convey the message, as it's shown. Often those things that may seem odd or completely out of context are those things that matter most to the one receiving the reading.

I have a dear friend who is a well-known psychic. She has given thousands of readings over the course of her lifetime. In her classes, she often tells the story of providing a reading for a woman whose husband had terminal cancer. Now, unlike me, she is okay with speaking to timeliness of death. Of course, the client asked her how long she had with her husband. My friend tuned in and saw a wonderful summer day. Trees were full of leaves. The grass was emerald green. The sun was high in the sky. There was a festive, happiness in the air as she saw the family gathering. Because she saw this wonderful scene, she put it together that her husband would be present at this family event and conveyed that to her client. Unfortunately, the client's husband passed quite a bit sooner than what she had predicted. After the death, the woman contacted my friend. More than anything, she wanted to understand why my friend saw what she saw. Of course, they went back and discussed the reading. It was uncovered that, indeed, there was a family reunion, but it was after the passing of the husband. The message was not that the husband was going to make it to that gathering, but that the family would make it through and come together in a happy and joyful way. It's a classic case of getting the right information, but the interpretation of the vision was off.

©istockphoto.com/sandramo

Frequently, visions are aligned with religious apparitions, but certainly are not exclusive to only that genre. However, they *are* frequently documented in history (i.e., Jesus' vision of a dove when being baptized in the Book of Mark). Within a religious vision, messages of inspiration and great hope are passed on. And it's not only Christians that claim visions. Various indigenous tribes worldwide utilize Shamans to guide their clans with the visions that they receive. Everything from finding food to starting war with another tribe can be influenced by a "medicine man's" (another word for Shaman) visions. Within the Aboriginal community, visions are quite normal. With the many groups that wander such a large, expansive piece of land, visions have become another form of communication within the tribes. Sending messages, through visions, of an ill family member or how a hunt for food is going, is very common.

Oftentimes, during a clairvoyant situation, symbols are given to the psychic receiver. For example, when I am asked what career path is best for a client, I may see a big, red cross. Now, this isn't meaning a life as a cleric, as some may perceive. I see this as a medical symbol and I know to communicate to my client that it's in his best interest to look into a health field. While the cross is a dominant Christian symbol, the more specific *red cross* (connecting lines all the same length) is a sign of the Red Cross medical auxiliary unit. What you need to remember, as a budding psychic, is that your interpretation of a sign or symbol will be unique to you, so it's a good idea to tell the client literally what you are seeing and then mention, to the receiver, what it means to you. The *smallest* amount of interpretation is best.

©istockphoto.com/Kriss Russell

Exercise

It may be very beneficial as you begin your psychic journey to take a list of words and jot down the first visual image that comes to mind. Let the list be completely random. Make sure to think of places, people, careers, emotions, family, etc. As you grow as a psychic, remind yourself of this list and use it, in combination with your other psychic "hits" as a guide to become more accurate in your readings.

Another form of clairvoyance is "remote viewing." Although it often stands alone when spoken about, remote viewing is the concept of someone projecting her mind to a far off, distance point/place and reporting back various and specific details of what was seen. Sometimes linked to astral travel (we'll talk about that later), remote viewing *may* be a form of clairvoyance where the psychic actually leaves the body to journey to another location. Various studies (particularly in the 1970s) performed by universities and the United States government ("Project Stargate" among others) came to the conclusion that remote viewing is absolutely possible and probable to receive information without any known physical connection.

Items that are shown to a clairvoyant psychic may vary. A vision might include a place and then very rapidly change to a date (perhaps being shown a calendar month) and then a face. What you have to remember is this: What means one thing to you, may mean something completely different to the person you are reading for. A pregnant woman, to you, may mean quite literally a birth of a child, but to another, it may mean adoption, a new business endeavor, etc. All things "birth" related come into play. A colorful maple tree may personally be seen as a symbol of Autumn, but to another it may be a memorial of someone who has passed. As you progress in your psychic development, you'll become more and more adept at realizing what things mean *for you* as well as what could potentially be a metaphor or symbol for the client.

©istockphoto.com/Luis Bellagamba

Clairaudience

Clairaudience IS ALSO A FRENCH word. It means "clear hearing." With clairaudience, the argument could be made that it is one of the tougher psychic abilities to *discern*. Learning this ability is quite easy, but often we struggle with it due to our own thought processes and memory. Sometimes, clairaudience is seen as another branch of clairvoyance, but I believe it to be its own, independent skill set and we'll take a moment to look at it that way. In Chapter 9, I'll give you some easy tips and techniques to help you utilize this psychic skill.

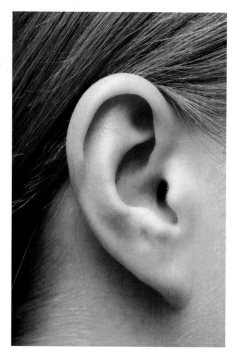

©istockphoto.com/MorePixels

Much like clairaudience, you may psychically hear something that is very literal or seemingly quite random. For instance, you may hear a church bell. In this case, you would likely think of a place of worship. But the meaning of this communication may just be a simple bell. What I have found in my own readings and studies of clairaudience is that what you hear is, at the core, the most basic explanation. Although you may hear a *church* bell, why wouldn't that just be a grand representation of a bell? Something ringing? It seems that, often, the universe (spirit guides, angels, etc.) will use the greatest form of what we need to receive. Because clairaudience often becomes confused with our own self-talk, I believe that the information needs to be conveyed in the most direct, "loudest" (I put this in quotes as it's not that we hear with our physical ears, but an inner voice) way possible.

As I mentioned above, clairaudience feels very much like inner dialogue. A big question that I hear from my students is that they struggle to differentiate their own thoughts and memories from what is being given to them clairaudiently. For right now, know that there is a difference. I'll work with you in a later chapter on how to distinguish everything. Clairaudience, much like clairvoyance, doesn't come through your physical ears. When you receive something, it's very much like recalling a speech or a line of dialogue from a movie that you have heard.

It's part of you, but not yours. In fact you may "hear" it as a different voice. Or, you may observe a clairaudient situation as you feel as if type was scrolling through your mind. Much like a ticker tape used in the 1930s, words that you could almost read run across your psychic mind.

It may be that you not only receive auditory messages from spirit, but the messages also may come from nature itself. Animals and plants often project and amplify messages. Understand this is not telepathy; they are actually reflecting the messages from the universe. It's a tough concept to understand, but one that you should be, at a minimum, aware of and familiar with. Often, these messages are a bit more ambiguous and might startle you at first. They frequently impress upon you a feeling, rather than giving you a direct message. It often feels like a gentle nudge to pay attention to something else that will be conveyed to you. Just having the knowledge that it *could* happen, is enough.

Another instance of a "vibrational," clairaudient message is receiving a message of song or hum. Personally, when I do too many readings, my ears plug up and I experience pressure and ringing in the ear. It's not painful or a discomfort, but it *is* noticeable. I know this to be a message, from the universe, that it's time to back off and give myself some rest.

A client of mine worked and struggled at developing her psychic abilities as a whole. She was very dedicated and definitely put in the time and effort that was and *should* be required to work on herself and her personal development.

It was only after working around the house where she started to *sing* (vibrational) that she noticed messages from her angels coming through. She was adjusting her own body's vibration by using her vocal chords to connect.

Various people in history have had documented clairaudient occurrences. Joan of Arc is a wonderful example of someone who made claims to hear not only the voice of her angels, but also St. Catherine and St. Michael. The Bible mentions over and over kings, prophets, and Jesus Christ himself hearing the "Voice of God." And it's not only Christian mythology that claims to hear a psychic voice. The Greeks told of muses that would "softly whisper" in the ears of artists to give them inspiration and creativity. Often, the resounding works would be dedicated to the muse for the insight and ambition that was needed to create such an accomplishment.

Another historical figure spoke about his personal "daimon" that was the "voice which, when it makes itself heard, deters me from what I am about to do and never urges me on." This man was Socrates. Quite frequently, Socrates would mention this voice that gave him inner strength. So often would he speak about this inner voice that his friends and peers would consult with him utilizing his clairaudient abilities. Not to be confused with the Christian "demon," a "daimon" is many things to many cultures. In this instance, Socrates found it to be his psychic hearing. For other cultures, a daimon was a deity in between men and God. In the Hermetic traditions, it was absolutely the same as an angel. I feel it is more of a nature spirit than a human one.

Of course, it is with due diligence that I need to speak to the idea of "bad voices." It's unfortunate that in our society if you make claims about "hearing voices," people most readily go to a psychotic or schizophrenic idea. And, sometimes, that is certainly the case. If those voices that you hear speak to you of anything negative, doubting, suicidal, or violent, you need to receive immediate professional, medical help. There is *never* any time where a light being (spirit guide, angel, or spirit) would ever convey to you to do anything harmful to yourself or others. You might receive information that is uncomfortable, but it will never be something that will put you in a place of hurt. That *is* an absolute.

©istockphoto.com/Oktay Ortakcioglu

Clairgustance

"CLEAR TASTING" IS THE MEANING of the French word *clairgustance*. Unlike clairvoyance and clairaudience, we find that with clairgustance, we actually taste things with our physical sense. It's as if a craving or an actual taste is in your mouth; however, it's not you, as an individual, that is having the desire. Because this is such an obvious knowing (we know if we are putting anything into our mouth or not), we can quickly register this as psychic activity if it happens to us. However, because it really is so apparent, we tend to dismiss it rather quickly. We'll reason that the flavor that we taste is an after effect of something we had eaten earlier, or perhaps write it off to a medication we're on.

An example of clairgustance is if you, full from a meal, were to walk into a friend's home. Upon entering the kitchen, you had an overwhelming sense or taste of blueberry muffins. Now, you have just eaten, you're not hungry, you're not smelling muffins baking, nor were you craving a muffin before walking into the home. However, much of your focus is about blueberry muffins. When you ask your friend about the muffins, you come to find out that only hours earlier, muffins were purchased at a local bakery for the family to enjoy for breakfast.

The term clairgustance is frequently used to cover two different psychic abilities. The other is called *clairalience* or *clairscent*. Both mean (from the French) "clear smelling." Because our senses of taste and smell are so closely related, it's easy to understand why one word is sometimes used to cover two, very specific psychic skills. Again, with the psychic smell, we do so with our physical nose. However, there is no physical reason to smell what we are receiving. For the sake of brevity, I'll use clairgustance to speak to both psychic taste *and* smell. Although I use the term to cover both, please note that they can certainly happen simultaneously, but do not necessarily have to.

©istockphoto.com/Skip ODonnell

My husband is an avid fisherman and frequently takes trips that keep him away from home for a long weekend or a few days. Albeit that we have a dog and cat that would alarm me to anyone at the front door, I still had a bit of hesitancy about being alone. As I was doing some housework one evening while he was out, I started thinking about my safety. I went around and made certain all the doors and windows were locked. But, despite my caution, I couldn't shake those silly feelings of unease. So, I said a little prayer to my angels to keep my family and me protected. Just *moments* after I had said my request to the divine, I received a sign.

All of a sudden my house filled up with the smell of warm, right out of the oven, apple pie. It was amazing. I first noticed it up in my bedroom, which is on the second floor of the house. Of course, I flew downstairs to the kitchen to make certain I hadn't *somehow* forgotten that I was baking something. Of course, nothing was there. I went all over my house again, checking to make sure all my windows were closed—that I wasn't picking up the smell of a neighbor baking. All the windows and doors, just like before, were secure. I *went outside* (being the good little paranormal investigator I am, looking for any way to debunk a situation) to see if I could smell anything out around my yard. Nothing. And for those of you skeptics out there, I didn't even have an "apple pie" candle in my house to give off that scent. I really went through my house. Of course, I finally understood that was a way the other side could immediately comfort me (nothing comforts me like food) and make me feel taken care of.

I truly believe that the most familiar way the other side communicates is through clairgustance. Think about it; having a taste or a smell is probably one of the *most* memory-provoking events that can happen to an individual. I know when I walk past people in a mall or the grocery store and they are wearing a certain cologne or perfume, I recall memories very quickly. I go right back to the past situation and remember the people I was with and how I felt at the time. Our sense of smell was our first sense that we developed as humans, so it's only right for us to be so attuned to it.

Also, tasting something or having a fragrance pass through quickly isn't *nearly* as startling as seeing someone appear before your eyes. Not that clairvoyance or clairaudience is necessarily scary, but it may take you off guard for a moment. Having a familiar smell or taste that is something subtle is really a blessing. It draws your mind back to the past, for a moment, to remember a time of comfort. And being so subtle, you can take the time to recognize the material, check for physical circumstances (if you can find any), and then, hopefully, allow yourself to feel comfort in the experience.

Now, there are times when you may smell or taste something negative. Remember, the first thing you must do is look for physical, traceable evidence of why this is occurring. In any situation, positive or negative, you don't want to automatically jump right to a paranormal or metaphysical answer. And remember, what may first come off as negative, may just be abnormal *to you.* It is really quite unlikely that a low level or negative energy is trying to impede you in any way. But, it does happen.

If you feel nauseated by the taste or smell, this is a sign that there may be something that is problematic. If you feel frightened, you need to know that you have domain over anything that comes in psychically or energetically. I recommend doing anything pious at this point. Say the Lord's Prayer. Ask your angels to come keep you safe and give you clarity around the situation. Whatever it may be to make you feel comfortable, but always remember; the bottom-line is that you can *tell* (don't ask) this to stop immediately. I don't want to frighten you, but with the positive comes the negative and we need to be educated about it all. We'll talk more about psychic protection in Chapter 7.

Clairsentience

Clairsentience IS THE FRENCH word (Are you seeing a pattern here?) for "clear feeling" or "clear sensing." I think it's best explained by the word "empathic," which I use as a synonym, often interchanging one word for another. An individual who has a predisposition to clairsentience frequently has an inkling about a situation. It's almost knowingness without any information or tangible evidence. There is just an understanding about an event or energy. And this knowingness may come through a gut feeling, an emotion, or a mood. As such, it's often very difficult to give specific information that a clairsentient person is receiving, as it's more about the impression around something than a direct piece of information.

We have to remember, with clairsentience, the entire body is the antenna for the psychic information. So, information may come in various forms. As I mentioned above, it's often a gut feeling or being compelled one way or another regarding a situation. But, it may also be displayed as a tickling or tingling sensation. Or, in another instance, you may feel a pressure at the top of your head or within your inner ear. All of these things are a clairsentient "hit." You can see where this type of information is much more vague, but that doesn't make it inaccurate. Clairsentience is the easiest psychic skill to develop, but certainly the most difficult to articulate and validate.

Have you ever gotten a strange feeling when walking into a room? Perhaps you were overtaken with grief. Maybe you just wanted to giggle. All these examples are clairsentient experiences. The psychic picks up whatever energy(s) that has transpired in the room. Unfortunately, for those not familiar with the experience, you may feel like it's *your* emotion and need to work through it. That's the greatest point to remember when working clairsentiently: The vibrations, good or bad, are *not* yours. They are only passing through you as a message. Allow yourself to be open to the experience, but always remain grounded knowing what is truly yours and what is the exchange of the communication.

Animals and children have a tremendous predisposition to being clairsentient. Animals have what we like to refer to as an "instinct" about where to go, where they are safe, and who they can trust. In the same manner, children are *very* good at an extremely young age with identifying who, they too, can rely upon and who will take care of them. Oftentimes they don't have the words to tell us why. They just have the reaction to someone who doesn't feel right to them. Isn't this, really, just a form of clairsentience? It's just an innate knowingness, without experience, about a person, place, or thing. On a side note, as children age, we often become less and less in tune with all of our psychic abilities as we are told what to believe, whom to trust, and how to behave. Not that these are bad things. But, we grow to rely on others to gauge for us what feels right. Later in time, we come back to trusting our intuition and then, hopefully, opening up our psychic awareness.

©istockphoto.com/Nicole S. Young

Many view psychometry as a form of clairsentient behavior. *Psychometry* (sometimes called psychic touch) is the term used when someone can pick up psychic energies and impressions from an intimate object. Joseph Rodes Buchanan, in 1842, coined the term (from the Greek words *psyche*, meaning "soul," and *metron*, meaning "measure") when he developed a theory that all things project energy. The projection of the energy may come in various ways. As it's frequently portrayed in the media, you can find numerous characters on various television shows having the ability to touch an item and either see the past, as related to the object, or the future of the person who owns the object. Most notably, the late Johnny Carson, playing the character "The Great Karnack" on the Tonight Show was a humorous portrayal of a clairsentient psychic.

Clairsentience is not just a subject for those interested in parapsychology; it is also mentioned in some religions. Buddhism, for example, believes that clairsentience is one of the six "spiritual penetrations" of humans. In other words, Buddhists believe there are six special gifts that human beings can achieve and one of them is the ability of clairsentience.

This ability can be obtained through a deeply advanced meditation level. In their terms, one is able to reach a point of feeling the "vibrations" of other people. Meaning the moods, thoughts, and ideas of an individual can be read, prior to articulating anything, by someone of superior concentration and centeredness.

©istockphoto.com/sandramo

Exercise

Take an object unknown to you in your hands. It may be keys from a friend or a coin that you find on a street. Hold it, or, if you prefer, hold your hands *over* the object. Allow your mind to clear and go blank. Then after a few minutes, ask the universe to show you notable information in regards to this object. Don't let anything go unrecognized. Look for a vision. Maybe there will be a specific emotion tied to the object. Perhaps a personal memory may be brought to you. Whatever it is, allow it to sink in and connect you deeper with the object. If the item came from a friend or person in contact, follow up with them. Share your impressions and look for validations in what you have received as a message from the session.

4

Psychic "Tools" of the Trade

THERE ARE VARIOUS DIVINATION "TOOLS" OUT THERE. Most are readily available. You can go into your local bookstore and find everything from a Tarot deck to a fortune-telling board. However, a downside to all of the new gear is the touting of the word *psychic*. Please remember that true psychics don't need an apparatus to gain insight. Now, don't get me wrong; there isn't anything wrong with using something external. But there is a semantics error when a Tarot reader calls himself a psychic.

There are many, many types of divination tools (specifically, physical and tangible tools that can help predict/show future or past events) that can awaken and/or assist our psychic abilities. Or we can simply make use of them, alone, to gather information about a situation. Whether it's utilizing the Tarot, dowsing (using a pendulum or dowsing rods), palmistry, numerology, or astrology (by no means is this the entire list), all of them are tried and true methods of delving within. No one method is better than another. Really, it's all about personal preference and what resonates with each individual. Let's touch on some of them now.

Tarot

TAROT CARDS ARE USED FOR divination purposes. The oldest partially surviving deck is from the 15th century, and unfortunately, only fragments are left. It's speculated that the Tarot deck was used as a simple game up until the 18th century, when it started being used to divine information. The first decks were hand-painted. However, in the late 1700s, the first Tarot deck was officially published. The divination aspect gained a broader popularity in the early 1900s due to the publishing of the Rider/Waite deck, which could be argued, is still the most popular Tarot deck (still in distribution) in the world.

As you can see, Tarot cards have a long history. The origin of the Tarot is quite questionable. No one is 100% certain about the origins of this 78 (typically) card divination deck. What we can say for certain is that it pre-dates our standard 52-count playing card deck (which is speculated to be an offshoot of the Tarot) and that deck is approximately 600 years old. A good point to note is that Tarot cards are different from oracle cards. Both are divination tools. An Oracle deck may have any number of cards where, as I mentioned above, a standard Tarot deck holds 22 Major Arcana (these are the trump non-suited cards) cards and 56 Minor Arcana (suit) cards equaling 78. An easy way to think of the Tarot deck is that it is similar to our playing card deck, just with extra "joker" cards.

Photo Credit: Donn Shy

Photo Credit: Donn Shy

Photo Credit: Donn Shy

The standard four suits of the Tarot are Cups, Swords, Pentacles, and Wands. Different decks may use different terminology, such as Crystals for Swords, Disks as Pentacles, and so on. This does *not* change the divination of the card. Each card has its own individual meaning. In a *very* general sense, cups represent relationships, both familial and romantic. Swords speak to external change around us, what we create that has an effect. Pentacles or coins divine information about work/career and money. Lastly, Wands are the internal changes we go through, giving insight on our emotions and our spiritual state.

Photo Credit: Donn Shy

Ultimately, the Tarot deck was created to show and foretell the typical human path. Using archetypes (standard situations that we, as people, go through) the querent can gain information by getting perspective on the situation, although unique to the individual, through the cards. Carl Jung (a famous psychologist) wrote extensively on the use of Tarot cards and the important symbolism therein. It's believed by many that the cards don't necessarily show you anything that you don't already know. However, it may only be on a subconscious level. By exploring and viewing the symbols on the cards, you can bring that knowledge, and potential insight into your future, to your conscious, waking self.

The cards are laid out in what is called a "spread." A Tarot spread may be very simplistic (one card) or several cards. There are an infinite number of spreads as, often, those who repeatedly use the Tarot create spreads "on the fly" so to speak, when a new query comes to be. Two common spreads are a three-card spread and a ten-card spread. The three-card spread is typically used as a "past, present, and future" spread—one card pulled for each facet of a situation. Hopefully, the three cards will show not only what led to the situation, but the probable outcome. Another typical spread is called a "Celtic Cross" and is covered in most beginner Tarot books. One that I recommend frequently is *Tarot: Plain and Simple* by Anthony Louis. The Celtic Cross spread uses 10 random (or not so random if you believe in the "fate" of the cards) cards placed in a certain way with each position being defined by a certain aspect of life. For instance, in a Celtic Cross spread, there are positions for not only past and future, but what is blocking a situation/person and the hopes and fears around the circumstances. Of course, the more cards you pull, the more in depth (and potentially more confusing) the reading can become.

Carl Jung, 1910

Celtic Cross Spread

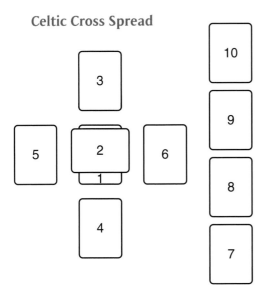

Within a spread, you may pull cards that are right side up or upside down. Upside-down cards are called "reversed" cards. There is much debate about whether or not to read reversed cards as they speak to the shadow, opposite, or negative side of a meaning of a card. The argument is that within *everything* there is good and bad and that neither should be isolated nor highly focused on. As human beings, we have free will and our conscious will determine what path we'll follow. Ultimately, if you choose to study and read Tarot, you'll decide what is right for you. Like everything else, this, too, is a personal preference.

There is a great deal of connection between the Tarot and other, alternate, divining methods. One of the most obvious is the Tarot's connection to numerology. Of course, with the suit cards being numbered within each suit, and the numbers 1-22 (or 0-21 depending on your preference) assigned to the Major Arcana, numbers are integral to the Tarot fundamentally. Working with the suit cards, you can apply basic numerological principles to each number. For instance, in the Tarot (much like our playing card deck) we have an Ace. So, really, it's a "one." A one in numerology represents newness and beginning. So, applying that to a card *and* a suit, an Ace in any suit would be a new endeavor in the "topic" of the suit. An example: An Ace of Wands (a suit in the Tarot) would speak to feeling new feelings or maybe seeing things from a new perspective.

If you choose to study Tarot and ultimately purchase a deck, remember to buy a deck that really speaks *to you.* I don't buy into the philosophy that everyone should start off with the Rider/Waite deck. Not that there is anything wrong with this deck (it, indeed, is very popular); however, I just think that you need to be vested in the symbolism that *you'll* be working with. If you don't resonate with the colors and pictures, you won't connect with the deck the way that you should. And that, ultimately, creates a tough learning situation. Remember, most decks are standard, so no matter what deck you choose, you'll be able to study from books and other resources out there.

Pendulums

PENDULUMS HAVE BEEN AROUND for thousands of years. The act of using a pendulum to gain information is called *dowsing*. Dowsing can be done, not only with pendulums, but also with divining rods (either man-made or natural). Often, in the past, people used this technique for finding underground springs of water. Utilizing a pendulum, you can dowse for future predictions, timing, yes or no answers, or even attempt to find water or missing objects. In addition, the pendulum is sometimes utilized in paranormal situations to become aware of extraordinary energies and potentially communicate with them. Ultimately, the idea is that every being holds and emanates positive or negative energies and utilizing that, information can be gained with the pendulum through dowsing. Just like radios pick up unseen audio waves, in the same way, pendulums can pick up alternate subtle energies.

Most often, a pendulum is held over a chart made by the user to gather insight into a current situation. The charts may be as simple as a "yes" or "no" or as complex as months, days of the week, or specific potential outcomes known by the one searching for information. For example, a pregnant woman looking to find out more information on the date of her child's birth may create what looks like a pie chart. Within each piece of the "pie," she would write numbers 1-31. Holding the pendulum over the chart, she could, with a steady hand keeping a fixed point, see where the pendulum swings most frequently.

Once there is a pattern with the pendulum "picking" a particular date, she would assume that her baby would be born on that day. Of course, this is just one example of usage. Honestly, you can dowse on any question you may have.

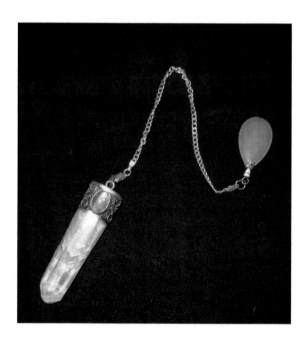

Pendulums come in all shapes and sizes. Some people prefer to make their own pendulum. (I'll tell you how in a moment.) You can also buy them at metaphysical shops. There isn't an absolute right or wrong way. Much like picking a Tarot deck, you have to do what feels right for you. Some pendulums are quite spectacular. Often made of crystals (amethyst, clear quartz, carnelian, etc.) with other stones embellishing the main stone, they can be quite expensive. On the other end of the spectrum, you can find simple, brass pendulums for under $10. Some believe that utilizing a pendulum of a certain material will assist in connecting to the energies that are being questioned.

As I mentioned above, you can make your own pendulum pretty easily. And, chances are, you'll have the supplies at home around you. Really, it only takes a piece of string or chain (whatever you prefer) and a weight. If necessary, you may need a ring/hoop/etc. to fasten the weight to the string. Oftentimes, people prefer to use a red string, but use what you have available. A weight may be a ring, heavy button, crystal, or charm.

Really, anything that can draw the string or rope tight will work. Once they are combined, a starter exercise for the newly created pendulum is to see how the pendulum calls out "yes" and "no" to the diviner.

Dowsing

To begin, you need to determine what is "yes" and "no" to your pendulum, whether it's homemade or newly purchased. Simply hold the top of the string of your pendulum in your dominant hand (typically the hand that you write with) with the pendulum not in contact with anything and ask the pendulum to show you "yes." The pendulum may swing left to right or up and down. Maybe it will rotate in a circular motion. Whatever happens, trust that this is the "sign" from your pendulum for "yes." In the same way, ask the pendulum the "sign" for no. Watch to see what direction the pendulum swings. Again, trust your answer for the "no." Now you're ready to start doing some dowsing!

From there, you can create your own charts to gain insight into whatever it is that you're looking for. You can create a chart that looks like a pie with as many "pieces" as you may need. Another concept is to create a chart that is made up of boxes. Think of a tic-tac-toe board that is closed in around all sides. Again, you can make as many squares as needed. Honestly, any way that you can conceive to make a chart is fine. What is important is that your energies are focused and guided to being open to receive information. The ways to dowse using a pendulum are infinite and only limited by your own imagination!

We find the idea of a pendulum even in religious services. You'll often see what is called a burning censer (incense burner) in churches that essentially is a large pendulum. This creates more of an atmosphere of prayerfulness, and is not necessarily used for divination; however, the similarity remains. The swinging of any object allows a mind to open and focus and perhaps connect better to the divine.

Of course, we all understand that the pendulum itself does not hold any magical divination powers. It's believed by those who use a pendulum that, ultimately, your subconscious and/or soul knows everything that you need to know about any given topic or circumstance. And, through the pendulum, that information can come. However, there is much controversy in the accuracy of dowsing with a pendulum. Several scientific studies have been performed world-wide (most notably in Germany and the Soviet Union); unfortunately, the studies did not prove that dowsing was accurate to anything above what could be predicted by chance. Of course, this doesn't mean that dowsing or utilizing a pendulum isn't worthwhile. It simply means that, like most divination tools, there may be unexplained nuances to using the pendulum.

I Ching

THE *I Ching* IS AN ANCIENT, classic Chinese text, also called the *Book of Changes*. The book, albeit a way of divination, is also seen by classical Chinese culture as a book of philosophy. It is, much like the Bible and the *Koran*, one of the most widely translated books in the world. Within the *I Ching* are definitions for 64 hexagrams. And in what combination you receive them will be your message. At the onset, the diviner, to receive information, used Yarrow stalks. However, as time passed, currency was invented and coins were more commonly tossed. In more recent times, Richard Wilhelm translated the *I Ching* (and was published for mass consumption in 1950) as well as other Chinese texts. Mr. Wilhelm's version is the most popular and most accredited translation to date.

©istockphoto.com/Tjasa Maticic

Based on Taoist philosophy, the *I Ching* works to describe how the universe does not have any coincidence or accidents. Its message is that everything happens, regarding both humans and nature, for a reason and it is meaningful and necessary. Although we may not understand the timing or the interaction, all is the way it should be and in perfect harmony. After the book was written (it's credited to Emperor Fu His who lived approximately 5,000-8,000 years ago), the great sage and philosopher, Confucius studied the *I Ching* and added 10 commentaries on it. They are seen as very valuable to its study and are often included as a foreword to the book, even today.

There are various methods for working with the coins. The diverse methods utilize different numbers of coins and tosses. The most common form of divination is taking three coins and tossing them three times to gather the hexagrams. With this method, you could gather over 4,000 answers without repeating. The coins used can be any type. Most notably, they must have a very clear "heads" and "tails." Some have even used such things as marbles, rice, and dice to work with the *I Ching*. The idea is not necessarily to predict the future with the *I Ching*, but to allow you to gain deeper insight into your own challenges and make better decisions because of that insight.

The *I Ching* (as well as Taoism itself) is actually based on the idea of balance in one's life. Ultimately, being a Taoist work (Taoism is both a religion and a philosophy based in Chinese culture), the point of everything written within the book is to be cognizant of experiencing the moment. And, within the moment, to remain balanced. From there, it is said, you can become enlightened. The concepts of "Yin" (dark space) and "Yang" (sunny place) are prominent within the *I Ching* as it's a firm Taoist belief. The idea of Yin and Yang is to understand the polarity within everything. No one thing is inherently good or inherently bad/evil. Each exists within one another to some extent.

There are several points to consider in asking the *I Ching* a question. In any reading, whether working with the *I Ching*, using Tarot, or getting a general psychic reading, it's *super* important to focus, put together, and phrase your question(s) quite specifically. I tell my clients "it's all about the question presented." First, remember to take the time to formulate a question, thinking about not only the topic, but if there is a timeframe involved and what you hope to accomplish. Next, be ready to receive an answer that you may not like or want. Finally, listen to the message that you receive. In the instance of using the *I Ching*, listen/read and really take into account what is told to you. Follow the instruction therein. I've read that, if given a choice on what route to take, *especially* with the *I Ching,* you should select the more difficult path as it enhances the soul's evolution. Really, what I think this means is that nothing of great benefit comes without diligence.

Another way to use the *I Ching* is to simply randomly open it every day and read the message (hexagram) that you turn to. Use this information as a study guide for the day. Or perhaps utilize the information in a daily meditation. It's believed that however you come to the message that you do, the universe ultimately destines it. In the vein that we, under any circumstance, get the message(s) that we need, in this way too we can gain insight.

The great psychologist, Carl Jung, intensely studied the *I Ching* and some give him credit for introducing the tool to the Western world. Dr. Jung's purpose for studying the book was to, hopefully, get a better grasp of the unconscious —a topic and theme that permeated Dr. Jung's entire career. Dr. Jung believed that this divination tool confirmed his synchronicity theory. His theory states that there is an underlying, unseen pattern in events that are seemingly random and coincidental. Because the *I Ching* could, within his opinion, quite accurately predict events or make suggestions that were quite poignant, showed him that truly, nothing was synchronistic.

Albeit Dr. Jung thought the *I Ching* to be quite accurate, others question the ability of a several thousand-year-old document to be predictive in present times. Proponents make the statement that if it wasn't a viable tool, it wouldn't have continued to exist. Others merely question the English interpretation of a Chinese book.

However, those critical of the *I Ching* make the claim that the hexagrams, although seemingly comprehensive, are quite vague. Much like a cold reading, the hexagrams could be poignant in almost anyone's life at a certain time. Nevertheless, I go back to what I mentioned earlier. Even if the hexagram is vague, even to the one in the situation in question, isn't it still exactly what we needed to hear in the moment? And isn't that, in and of itself, the entire basis for the *I Ching* at its core?

Palmistry

Palmistry, OTHERWISE KNOWN as "hand analysis" or "chiromancy," is a method of divination determined by the shape, creases, mounds, and lines in the palm of the hand. It has its roots in India beginning over 5,000 years ago. In fact, palmistry is mentioned in the Old Testament (Job 37:7 "He seals the hand of every man, that all men may know His work."). The ancient Hindus are credited with the conception of palmistry. The tradition has been carried on over the years to present time. Palmistry, like various other long-lasting divination tools, has had continued interest as people, especially in this fast-paced life, continue to search for answers beyond the commonly seen.

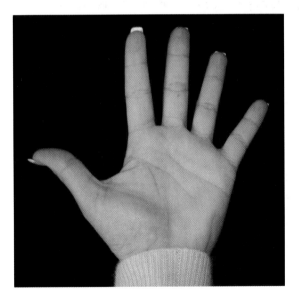

The history and roots of palmistry is varied and lengthy. As mentioned above, the practice has been in place for over 5,000 years. However, there is evidence of even earlier studies of the hand and palm. Pictures of the human hand have been found from the Stone Age, implying that even then, the hand was considered to have great importance worthy of documentation. There are also mentions of palmistry in China (around 3,000 BC) and in Egypt. It's thought that the Egyptians were the ones that passed palmistry along to the Greek nation where, ultimately, Aristotle wrote a book about it, it is reputed, for Alexander the Great. From there, the gypsies, who were thought to have originated in India, spread the practice through Europe going door to door or setting up tents in local towns and villages.

Cheiro

Later in the 19th century, a famous palmist named "Cheiro" (his true name was William John Warner, but he also went by Count Louis Hamon, claiming noble ancestry) emerged. Late in his teenage years, he made the choice to leave England and go to India where he was taught by an Indian Brahmin (Hindu teacher) the art of palmistry. Roughly two years later, Cheiro returned back to London where he provided readings and continued his studies for the next 40 years. In addition to his palmistry, he also claimed to be clairvoyant, as well as provided astrological and numerology readings. He spent his last years in Hollywood, with much success due to celebrity-requested readings.

Like many other divination tools, palmistry has various methods. In addition, much like Tarot, there are varied definitions for fixed points. Thus, palmistry can get a little confusing. What you need to remember when studying is to use what works and feels right *for you.* If you don't relate to a certain thought or process, then only take it in as education. Don't make it part of your doctrine. Ultimately, the location of the major lines and mounts are the same no matter what course of study you choose. It's the interpretation that may be inconsistent.

Traditionally, the fingers play a major role in palmistry. And, in most studies, the messages for them remain similar. The index finger is related to the planet Jupiter and speaks to leadership. A long index finger speaks to independent thinking, confidence, and strong judgment. Of course, a smallish index finger would mean the opposite. The middle finger is related to Saturn. This finger represents knowledge and wisdom.

Also, it defines the need for materialistic items in one's life. Typically this is the longest finger; however, if it is extraordinary long in comparison to the other fingers, it denotes a very strong ability to concentrate and focus. The ring finger is associated with Apollo/Sun. The ring finger relates to the creativity as well as growth and expansion of an individual. Here, too, luck and fame is shown. Ordinarily, the ring finger should be about the same length as the index finger, but, if it's shorter than the index finger, it may be a sign of someone who may be self-involved. Next, we have the "pinky" or last finger. Associated with Mercury, the smallest finger shows how an individual may communicate with others. If this finger is unusually bent or unusually straight, you can tell how honest the person may be. Through study and providing palmistry readings, you'll be able to judge what is extraordinary on a hand or more typical.

The thumb, in palmistry, is regarded by many as the most important part of the palm. Palmists pay special attention to the shape, angle, nail shape, and lines that make the thumb unique. It's thought that the thumb reveals the most about the character and personality of the individual. As the thumb contains the radial nerve that runs all through our bodies (spine and into the brain), palmists connect the thumb to reasoning and success. A thumb close to the fingers in the hand is a sign of a closed off and possibly shy personality, whereas a thumb that is more open shows a person who is more relaxed.

As with other readings, various issues can be covered in a palmistry reading. What palmistry excels at is the ability to tell you how to better your process. This makes it possible to not only gather information about the future but also to get a better idea of personal interactions. Learning how you relate to others, innate talents, and the paths of least resistance can benefit anyone and everyone. Unlike most other readings, you can take time to really learn about you. Often, subject matter comes to light that may not even be seen by the individual, which can make a palm reading quite worthwhile. And, as a person ages, the hand will change, which can make it beneficial to follow up with readings to see where our free will has taken us.

As I mentioned above, there are various contradictions in the meanings of different aspects in palmistry. Because readers take their own liberties with reading palms, it's hard to find any tangible evidence of accuracy. What may mean something to one reader, may mean something entirely different to another reader. As such, you can't make a base line study as to the accuracy. Now, the medical community has studied the aspects of the hand in regards to diagnosing certain health/medical issues. In these studies, there has been correlation between certain subtle changes in the palm, but the medical community in no way has supported the idea that the hand would conclude anything substantial about the character of a person.

Numerology

*N*umerology IS THE STUDY of numbers, with the understanding that each and every number has its own energy and value beyond the numerical connotation. With this comprehension, you can work to divine certain aspects about an individual. Conceptually, numerology is based on the idea that the universe is mathematically constructed and therefore aligns itself with numbers. In kind, we can reduce every letter in the alphabet to a numerical value, and here too, with the use of names, places, etc. gain insight into those things as well.

The history of numerology is debated. Some believe that the origins began in ancient Babylonia. However, it's Pythagoras (the Greek mathematician) that most give credit to. Although there are different schools of numerology (Chaldean, Kabbalah & Western, or Pythagorean), Pythagoras's system is most popular. He is called the father of numerology. Pythagoras believed that numbers hold vibrations that bring us closer to the universe and as such, those vibrations would be coded through the use of numbers. And through the vibrations, he believed, we can connect with the energies that impact future events.

Numerology is based only on single digit numbers. Any double, triple, etc. numbers should be added together and deduced into a single digit. For example, the number "35" would not be considered in numerology. You would add 3 + 5 to gain a value of 8 and that would be the numerological value. However, Pythagoras believed that some numbers should not be broken down. The numbers 11, 22, and 33 are all classified as "master numbers," meaning that they require more effort and study than just the single numbers. 11 is seen as the most mystical of the master numbers. It is the "psychic" number working on insight and knowingness without external knowledge. 22 is the melding of spirit with determination and grounding. Sometimes referred to as the "master builder," 22 combines the dreamer with the will and the focus to make things happen. 33 is the number that offers itself to the world—giving up oneself for the greater good of all. It's said that Jesus Christ was a master number 33. Compassion and self-sacrifice are the keys for 33.

The meanings of the single-digit numbers are very much based on the path that we, as humans, walk through life. I often think of the numbers in a diagram of climbing a mountain and coming down the other side. Using that analogy, let's briefly talk about the energies around every number.

ONE represents new beginnings. You're just starting the climb. You're excited, but unsure as to what this challenge will bring you. There's newness in the undertaking as well as the equipment. You're on your own, independent.

TWO is representative of duality. You have started your climb, but you're thinking about anything that you may have forgotten. You wonder if you're strong enough *for* the climb. But from here you become very adaptable. Be imaginative, centered, and balanced.

THREE is knowledge. You have found your stride. You have made it halfway up the mountain and are excited at the accomplishment. You have realized that you are able to multitask and find balance. The only downside is that you don't want to become too egotistical.

FOUR brings focus. You set aside the ego and really put your nose to the grindstone. You're almost to the top of the mountain. You become very practical and stable only working to achieve your goal, enlightened to the path that you've taken.

FIVE is the pinnacle of freedom! You have reached the top of the mountain and even though you may be exhausted, you have *much* energy! Optimistic about what is to come, you are not only excited for the journey down the mountain, but looking forward to documenting it.

SIX represents what I like to call the "Whew!" factor. You are pleased with what you have done. You were successful in what you wanted to achieve. At this point you may be a bit over-emotional, so remember that. You look forward getting back and spending time with your family.

SEVEN is all things spiritual. Your connection with the divine is deeper as you get closer to the base of the mountain. You reflect on things that you have learned and ponder the reason of it all. You find that you feel a connection with your soul that you haven't felt before. While you ponder, don't become unapproachable.

EIGHT is represented with clarity. You look back and reflect on what worked and what didn't. You have become very practical and start planning for the next trip, or, how you would do it differently.

NINE is finality. Completion. You have reached, once again, the base of the mountain. You feel healed by what you completed. But as you are thankful and proud, remember not to be too possessive or self-involved. Enjoy your journey and encourage others to begin theirs.

Now that you understand how the numbers hold value beyond just counting, you can look within and start to utilize them to discover more about yourself and others. What you'll find below is how to calculate your "Life Power" number. This number represents the strengths that you have in life that should guide you through various situations. Its value is figured by using your full first (whatever is on your birth certificate) and last name as well as your birth date. Every letter in the alphabet has its only numerical value. Here is a chart for the values for each letter:

1 = A, J, and S   2 = B, K, and T
3 = C, L, and U   4 = D, M, and V

5 = E, N, and W   6 = F, O, and X
7 = G, P, and Y   8 = H, Q, and Z

9 = I and R

So, you combine all things and add everything up, then break down the number to a single digit. An example (using my information) is below:

T I F F A N Y J O H N S O N =
2+9+6+6+1+5+7+1+6+8+5+1+6+5 = 68 =
6+8 = 14 = 1+4 = 5

7/25/72 = 7+2+5+1+9+7+2 = 33 = 3+3 = 6

5 (name value) + 6 (birth date value) = 11 = 1+1 = 2

Two, in my instance, is my life power number. This means that I need to remember not to take too much time making a decision or to act too quickly in any situation. I need to focus, throughout my life, to make decisions wisely and surround myself with those who can help in those decisions.

Crystals

CRYSTALS, I HAVE TO ADMIT, are one of my favorite things. I've been a "rock hound" since I was a young child. One of my favorite memories is diving for stones, around the age of seven, with a friend, in the lake that I grew up on. I frequently get asked if I truly believe in the energies of stones and if they can help develop abilities, psychic or otherwise. The answer is absolutely. I have felt it physically and psychically. If you concentrate, you'll feel the vibrations of stones. Whether it is a stone that you simply find on the ground on a hike, or one you come across at a metaphysical store, you can connect with stones and crystals. Some of my friends, who have said they are "psychic as a brick," have been able to feel the energies that stones emit. Fortunately, we live in a society where stones from around the Earth are readily available. We don't have the limitations to work with only the stones in our geographic area.

Typically, the colors of stones can give you a quick idea about what vibrations the crystal or stone may carry. As a general rule, the color of the stone often coordinates with one of the seven major chakras that are associated with it. (Chakras are energy wheels we have within our energetic body. We'll talk more about chakras in the next chapter.) For example, a blue stone will often work with the third-eye chakra and assist with psychic development. Blue stones include blue kyanite, lapis, or sodalite. Another example is reddish stones working with the root chakra. The root chakra is based on family issues as well as grounding. Stones for this chakra are carnelian and ruby.

Exercise

You may want to study a stone or crystal and develop a personal insight into the vibrations. If you feel drawn to a particular specimen, hold it in your dominant hand. Cover the hand holding the stone with the other hand, ultimately cupping the stone. Take a moment to clear your mind and see what information comes through to you. You may feel an emotion. There may be an image that comes to mind. If that happens, determine what that image means to you and how it makes you feel. Be aware of any physical responses you may have. Perhaps the stone feels light in your hand. Maybe you feel a tickle or pinch in your hand. Become conscious of any messages that are passed along to you from the stone. Know that these messages are *yours* whether or not they are validated by any crystal or stone book. As we all have different tastes for food, so do we have different responses to stones.

More specifically, there are stones and crystals to work with various issues or points where you'd like to see some growth. Everything from psychic development to losing weight to pregnancy can be addressed. Of course, when working with stones, the change can be subtle. There is never any substitution for going to a doctor for a physical malady. Below is a list of stones and crystals with the vibrations associated with them. Of course, this is not an exhaustive list as the number of stones is infinite. In fact, different crystals are being uncovered every day!

Amethyst: This is a beautiful, semi-precious stone that is often used in jewelry. Its color is purple, and it is the birthstone for February. Aligning it with your crown chakra, this stone helps in connecting with the divine. In addition, this stone is often called the "sobriety stone," as it also assists with chemical dependency issues.

Apatite: This stone comes in various colors, but is most commonly seen in a blueish, teal color. Not commonly known, this stone works on maintaining physical body weight by curbing your appetite. If you're working on keeping to a diet and exercise regimen, this is the stone for you! Also, it works with the heart chakra by allowing you to see *why* you are where you are in your life.

Bloodstone: As the name implies, this stone works with the blood in the physical body. It can work on the circulation of the body as well as blood pressure. This is a green stone with red flecks within it. It's a stone of bravery and courage, working on any fears that we may have from this or past lives. Along with everything else, this stone, too, assists with the heart chakra, balancing all energies through the heart.

Carnelian: This is a reddish/orange stone that works with the root chakra, bringing grounding and clarity in complicated situations, especially on the home front. In addition, it works to remove depression and protects against fear and jealousy. It can work to give you luck in the theatrical arena if that is your profession or passion.

Calcite: Calcite comes in many varied colors. Sometimes it's transparent; other times it's opaque. It's found in pink (a personal favorite), blue, yellow, orange, etc. Because of the many colors, it works to balance and clear all energies within the body. Use this stone if your circumstances are getting too serious or intense as it can bring humor and light to a situation.

Diamond: A wedding/romance favorite and the birthstone for April, the clear diamond (diamonds also come in a host of other colors including pink and blue) is really known as the "king" of crystals and stones. Diamonds resonate with the crown chakra and activate the other chakras creating a bond between the physical body and the soul.

Hematite: A favorite for banishing and dispelling negativity, this stone has a unique gray color with a mirror-like sheen. This stone is a wonderful stone to take to the office in corporate situations. It assists in focusing your energy and drive and works to bring peace around the holder. Because of its magnetic properties, it's said that this stone, too, is wonderful for circulation.

Iolite: In my opinion, iolite is one of the most beautiful stones. This stone is often seen in jewelry and considered "semi-precious." Connecting us with our third-eye chakra, this stone can help us in psychic development. What's special about this stone is that not only do we open up to our psychic selves, but also it helps to lessen fear around doing so.

Jade: Considered one of the most precious and revered stones in Eastern culture, you'll find it prevalent in jewelry with an Asian vibe. Coming in many colors including green, purple, and yellow, this stone is considered lucky by many. Aligning with the heart chakra, this stone allows you to, release negativity that you may perpetuate about yourself.

Lapis: This amazing blue stone was greatly valued in Egyptian culture. Aligning your energies with the third-eye chakra, this stone is probably utilized (outside of jewelry) for enhancing your psychic abilities. In addition, this stone can assist with manifesting your dreams and goals into reality.

Malachite: Malachite is a great stone to work with if you want to find the answers for why you are the way you are or why you do what you do. Giving insight and information on your own process, this stone works with the heart chakra. If you worry or stress about travel, this stone is a great one to bring with you to ease that fear.

Moonstone: One of the most mystical-looking stones, this smoky/cloudy stone is very connected with the moon (hence the name) and the divine feminine. This is a stone of "feeling;" however, it helps balance the emotions as well as understand where they are coming from. Moonstone also assists with connecting to your intuition and being able to acknowledge the wisdom within.

Obsidian: This black stone is a wonderful stone for repelling negativity. However, only work with obsidian if you are willing to address your own fear and negativity that you have within as it works to mirror your own issues for you. This stone is wonderful for healing either yourself or to use when healing others.

Opal: The October birthstone looks, in all its forms, like there is a fire inside each stone. This stone is a stone of inspiration. If you're trying to gather your gumption to do something and take a leap, this stone is for you. In addition, this stone can help you when trying to accept change in your life. Allowing you to see the "silver lining" in every situation.

Pearl: From the sea, we get the pearl. As June's birthstone, we have energies that help us with "pregnancy." That could mean the very literal pregnancy with a child, but also the energies of all creation. So, if you're looking to start a new business or create a new endeavor on any level, this is the stone for you. Also, the pearl is *very* good for digestive issues.

Peridot: August's birthstone resonates with the heart chakra assisting matters of love and relationships. The claim has been made that this stone is very protective; as such, it can create a shield of protection around the body. It's recommended that if you wear or carry peridot on you, remove it before doing any healing work.

Quartz: Quartz comes in a bunch of varieties. From smoky to rose quartz, it provides energy to the user. That's the cornerstone of quartz: energy. In any form, this stone directs and focuses energy where you need to project it. It amplifies energy and thoughts. So, it's a wonderful stone to build ESP. This is, for most, the building block of stone and crystal studies.

Ruby: The ruby is July's birthstone. Also a stone that resonates with the root chakra, the ruby is known for bringing material prosperity. As such, it's been a favorite for royal families and is often seen in noble jewels. Ruby brings you out of a place of victimization, showing an individual the goodness of their works.

Sapphire: A quite visible semi-precious stone that is often seen in jewelry. Resonating with various chakras due to the many colors it comes in, September's birthstone allows one to open the mind and gain insight. Great for working on mental clarity, it also assists in defeating depression. I know that if I received a sapphire, I'd cheer up!

Sodalite: Not to be confused with lapis (as they look somewhat similar, both being blue), sodalite also resonates with the third-eye chakra. It can increase the understanding of psychic information that you may receive. Further, it can help you really solidify the qualities that you may be looking for in a relationship, romantic or otherwise.

Tigers Eye: Tigers eye is one of my favorite stones. Its fluctuating brownish color holds the energies of both Sun and Earth. It is a stone of protection and gives you extra strength and stamina. Working with the solar plexus chakra, it shows you your personal needs that you may be ignoring. Also a very lucky stone.

Unakite: Both pink and green in the same specimen, this stone resonates with the heart chakra. What's special about this stone is that its energies help you go past physical symptoms and see the source of any health issues, looking and drawing you to the emotional causes of disease. Also this stone is great to assist with childbirth.

As you can see, there are stones for everything and anything. As I mentioned earlier, using stones is not a substitute for working with a doctor or trained professional. Crystals and stones *definitely* have their own, unique energies, but they are often soft and caressing. They are meant to assist us where we may have a weakness or lack. There are many books published *just* on the meanings of stones, not to mention the application(s) of them. I encourage you to work with them!

There are many, many books published on crystals and stones. Whether you would like to learn more about the mineral makeup or metaphysical and spiritual properties, various information abounds. One book that remains to be held in the highest of standards is *Love is in the Earth; A Kaleidoscope of Crystals* by Melody. This book incorporates not only the metaphysical properties, but also speaks to the astrological signs associated with the stones as well as colors and growth patterns.

What Else

NOW THAT I'VE INTRODUCED several divination tools, I'd like to share some other psychic subjects that integrate with development. Where, in the prior chapters, we had tangible things to look at and use, the following topics aren't quite so concrete. What we'll focus on here is more the esoteric and subjective. Everything from intuition to astral projection is what you make of it. Albeit we *can* validate what we receive, it may be a bit more of a stretch to utilize these objectives. But, like anything else, don't worry. When you begin anything, there is a learning curve. Don't become distracted or discouraged. No one starts off an expert and *no one* has 100% success the first time working with new material.

When I came back to my metaphysical roots as a young adult (I had wonderful experiences as a child and studied young, but pulled back a great deal in my late teens), I had some pretty terrific experiences and found that some things came quite quickly and aptly. However, after having a bit of success, the "flow," if you will, stopped. Just shut down. Everything went quiet. *That*, my friends, was scary. I went from crying (literally) about what was happening to me to crying for what was *not* happening! Finally, the fear went away and I sat down and meditated with a clear head. The message that I heard was this: As you grow psychically, your physical body needs to evolve as well as to be able to handle the energies. So, if you have a similar experience of things "turning off," don't sweat it. It's your physical body being given the time to catch up to your aura, etheric, and energetic self! Using a divination tool, you have something to lean on. These next few concepts are all for you!

Intuition

I GET MANY QUESTIONS regarding how intuition is different from psychic ability. Let's address that right away: Psychic ability comes from outside your own body from another source, whereas intuition is really that "gut" feeling and stems from inside of you. A wise soul once told me that there is divine light, from the source, within each one of us to guide us home. Think of it as our personal North Star. The light inside us (personally, I envision it as a little candle in my belly) is where intuition is seated and, ultimately, communicates our wisdom.

The true definition of *intuition* is knowing something without realizing you know it. Intuition is often linked with psychic ability, even though it is something quite separate. However, a strong intuition may be a sign of a strong psychic ability. Frankly, if you can pick up on subtle messages from within, you may have an innate predisposition to keen psychic ability. What you have to remember about your intuition is that it's knowingness about something without ever *thinking* about it.

Probably the best example of intuition is what mothers have for their children. Of course, we're talking about *mother's intuition*. Who hasn't heard the story of a mother knowing that her child was in danger? My mother, who I don't believe would call herself psychic, but is awfully intuitive in her own right, had concern for my little brother driving. Of course, all moms worry about their children in cars and car accidents.

However, on one particular day, my mom had that gut feeling of apprehension, but it was multiplied by 10. So much so that in her worry, she made my father discontinue a phone conversation he was on. Moments later, she got the call that, in fact, my brother *had* been in a car accident coming home from work. Fortunately, he wasn't badly hurt. This is the perfect example of intuition. My mother had NO *knowingness* of my brother's accident, but yet she *knew* within herself that it had happened.

Some people have an inclination to different types of intuition. While as many types of intuition could occur as people, we'll touch on a couple specialties. First, let's discuss *medical intuition*. There are some individuals who feel they have intuitive strength toward health concerns. Although they rarely are trained in the medical field, they seem to be able to either diagnose various symptoms or find the root cause of a health issue. Another specific form of intuition is *mathematical intuition*. Although the term is called "mathematical intuition," the idea works around any sort of problem-solving scenario.

Say, for instance, that a person is working through a problem. It could be as simple as getting from point "A" to point "B". She already knows the solution; however, she is lacking in the knowledge of how to get there. Perhaps she isn't familiar with the area, but has a general idea of the geography. All of a sudden, in a moment of calm, she sees the solution and the steps to get there. Now, perhaps she has tried variations of the steps but hasn't been successful. But now, for some reason, she just *knows* that the procedure that she has now discovered is the solution. Even if it doesn't make logical sense. And, upon doing the work, she finds that she was correct and determines a route to get to her location, although she wasn't aware of the way.

There's a lot of debate about the distinction between intuition and instinct. Although they may stem from the same place and more than likely developed simultaneously, there are pretty significant differences. First, I believe that instinct is more action oriented. For instance, if a rattlesnake rattles at us, we understand the meaning without ever having been bitten. If we approached a tiger and it growled at us, we would back away. Instincts are very much about survival and keeping ourselves safe. Conversely, intuition is more about you and what's best for us. It's not about life or death, but it's about what's in our best interest on a day-to-day basis. Intuition is going to give us information about things such as relationships, timing out certain situations, our career, and finances—not what berries are poisonous.

Solar plexus chakra symbol

The chakra (discussed in detail later in this chapter) that is most associated with intuition is the solar plexus chakra. This chakra, aligned with the color yellow, is seated right by our stomach. Subsequently, and I don't think it's coincidence, it's the same place that we associate with our "gut" responses to something. Other things that are housed in this chakra are self-esteem, social aptitude, who we are as an individual, and ego. To bolster this chakra, if you're working on developing your intuition, you can carry citrine or amber simply on your person whether it be in your pocket or, for example, around your neck as a pendant. Citrine, in addition to assisting the solar plexus chakra, is also known for bringing abundance and prosperity to the holder. Another "stone" that is beneficial is amber. Amber isn't really a stone; it's hardened sap from trees. Its metaphysical properties include bolstering intuition, healing, and providing psychic shielding.

Something to remember when you are working with and developing your intuition is that there isn't any emotion attached with intuition—another distinctive piece that is different from psychic information. Your intuition is going to speak to you very matter of factly. It's going to give you information that is subtle and honest. And frankly, sometimes our best interest is *not* what we'd like. Because this is the case, you will feel very neutral to the information given to you. You may feel that it's more something to consider rather than react to. Intuition gives us perspective; it's up to us how we choose to act.

A wonderful example of the neutrality within our intuition is using your intuition to get the best parking spot when out shopping. Ultimately, your parking spot will not have a terribly positive or negative effect on your life. It's a convenience that we all like to have and can really only benefit us by making us more efficient getting in and out of the store. Ask your "intu" when you should go run your errands to get the best parking. Listen and see what you hear from within. Then, act upon what you receive. Set the intention that when you show up to the store/shop you'll get the closest spot possible. It's a wonderful way to check your accuracy without engaging another individual. Remind yourself of results when utilizing your intuition in other situations.

Hopefully this helps you work with your intuition as *well* as your psychic abilities. Although they are different, they certainly can work together and there are things you can do to bolster both. Remember that intuition is *inside you.* I frequently hear from those who feel next to no psychic ability that their intuition compensates a great deal. Think of your intuition as your personal, internal "magic 8 ball" that is with you at all times. Ask your intuition questions and see what you receive. You may get a "no" or you may get an "Ask again later." Either way, you've received information and will be better off listening to it.

Channeling

Channeling IS COMMUNICATING with an individual's spirit guide. Personally, channeling is the basis of my psychic practice. 90% of my clients ask me to speak to their spirit guides. That's what I call channeling. For others, it may mean something different. For some it means communicating with spirits. Others believe that you need to go into a trance like or altered state. Some people who channel find their bodies taken over by another spirit. There is vast debate on whether or not that is beneficial, but what is right for one, isn't, and doesn't have to be, right for another.

My "process" is predominately speaking with the spirit guides that everyone has. I don't go into a trance or lose consciousness in any way. My voice doesn't change, my eyes don't flutter. In fact, it's just like speaking with anyone. It's a conversation. I start out setting my intention to communicate, asking my client's guides to come through and simply wait for it to happen. Sometimes it may take moments; other times, for me, it may take a minute or two. I may hear them. I may see them. Oftentimes, when initially connecting, I feel them before any communication comes through. It may feel like I'm being watched. Or the energy in the room will become more dense. But, for you it may be something completely different. That's the key. As no one would ever describe a simple oak tree the same way, so it is with channeling. Everyone does it differently, but no one is wrong. It's simply your style.

I sometimes get asked how I perceive or see the "entity" after the connection has been made. Honestly, it's varied. Most often, the entity will look as if it's simply a being of light. I know it sounds silly, but the soul looks like a big, glowing amoeba. There have been instances where I see a spirit that looks very human; I'll get detail such as the pattern of a shirt, the nature of a smile, or the shape of a face. It really all depends. I think that, like the messages given, it may depend on the situation. For some it may be about hearing the message. It may not be necessary for an entity to show me the physical characteristics that he had when here on Earth. For others, it may be *very* important to let me know that they look similar on the other side. In the case of a violent or abrupt passing (for example, a car accident) the entity may want me to know that he has healed. That those injuries did not transfer over.

When channeling, it's the messages that can be most confusing. Frequently, a person will acknowledge the connectedness of feeling another spirit, but the communication can be sketchy. Remember, the other side vibrates very quickly, and the messages won't be straight, continuous sentences. The other side has to slow down a great deal to be able to speak with us here in the physical realm. You may, for example, psychically hear the word "red" then see a truck and the calendar month of November.

Now, some would say it's your job to find the context for the message, but I find that may be leading. So, I try to simply communicate exactly what I get. You'll not only be truer to your gift, but also truer to your client. What you'll find out, as you strengthen your channeling skills, is that you'll see certain symbols that mean specific things, but are not the literal meaning of what is being shown. For instance, you may see a maple tree with its colors changing. The message may not be about the tree; it is more likely a symbol for autumn.

As I mentioned, channeled messages can be about anything. Messages may be very ambiguous and vague. However, that doesn't make them any less relevant. Remember, you are *only* the tool that the message is coming through. You can't control the message. If something comes through that doesn't immediately place, there may be good reason for that. And it's nothing to concern yourself with. You cannot force what you receive. Sometimes people may only need to know a certain part of information instead of an entire message. You have to remember that the universe knows exactly what any individual needs at any moment in time. However, some messages may be very specific giving dates, names, and situations. Either way, trust in what you get!

On very rare occasions, what I perceive to be an angel will communicate. It's a very rare scenario. When channeling an angel (and I can only speak from my experience) it's more vibrational and often gives me a feeling of lightness, and I'll often get "goose bumps." When communicating with that high of an entity, it's not so much about the direct words. More accurately, I am, what I call, "impressed" with information. It's not a conversation, but a great knowingness about a situation that is in question and it happens in a split second. It's very much as if you were part of the experience and not only had your perspective, but the perspective of all those involved. That, along with the details such as climate, number of people, and other pertinent information; it's extensive.

There are many cultures and societies that work with those who channel. In many indigenous tribes/clans there are shamans, medicine people, and elders who are relied upon to connect, and ultimately communicate, with spirit(s). Tribes from all over the world utilize these channelers. Different people have different traditions. Some shamans go on a vision quest, oftentimes utilizing the physical rhythm and beating of a drum, then, they go within themselves to create a meditative state, to venture deep into the Earth and bring back information to the other members. Medicine men have been known to take substances to put them in an altered state. Through this state, they will sometimes receive visions or speak with the other side. Here again, as with the shaman, they may speak to the state of the clan or an upcoming war. The messages are endless.

As you can see, channeling is more about the personal experience. Everyone will have his own way and process. Again, what happens for you may be very different from what happens with another. There is no question in my mind that everyone *can* learn to channel and work to communicate with the other side. We'll talk about technique in a later chapter.

©istockphoto.com/Dan Brandenburg

Mediumship

MEDIUMSHIP IS DIFFERENT from channeling. But the process is quite similar. *Mediumship* is the communication with someone you can identify (either through the client or the psychic) and have a connection with, who has crossed over. For instance, a mother, father, or former co-worker. Mediums are conduits between the corporeal soul and the incorporeal. As I mentioned before, one of the most famous mediums is probably the Witch of Endor from biblical times. She was able to conjure up the spirit of Samuel at the request of King Saul. Samuel's soul came through to the two of them and spoke to King Saul's downfall. King Saul then died the next day in battle.

It's important to note that not all psychics are mediums. However, all mediums *are* psychic. Some psychics only feel that they connect with spirit guides, energies, and/or angels, none of whom have had a present, known life with you. (We'll talk more about how our spirit guides are connected with us in an upcoming chapter, but it's widely regarded that we, most likely, have had a *past* life with them at some point.) As such, some psychics don't claim mediumship as one of their working skills. However, by definition, a medium is connecting with an energy that is outside of them, and as such, that is the definition of psychic ability. Hopefully that's not too confusing. I do believe, that like any other psychic skill, mediumship can be learned as well.

Those involved in psychic research typically group mediumship into two different, unique groups: mental mediumship and physical or trance mediumship. *Mental mediumship* (which is the category I fall into) is the use of a psychic ability (clairaudience, clairvoyance, clairsentience, or clairgustance) to connect with a spirit and receive messages for clients connected to the soul. Mental mediumship is probably the most validating of the two as the psychic is receiving information that can be readily confirmed. *Physical mediumship* is allowing a spirit to come through; however, the spirit is communicating through different means. Often they will bang doors, move objects, and the like. Table tipping (which was very prominent in the late 19th century) was a demonstration of physical mediumship.

Although mediumship is still very popular, there are those who dispute its validity. Let me address the most obvious. In physical mediumship, objects can be rigged to move or make noise on demand. There are infinite sounds or theatrical demonstrations that can be produced. Regarding the act of mental mediumship, in this day and age of technology, there are many details that we can research and find out about individuals. Living or dead. Because of the *opportunity* for these activities, some skeptics immediately dismiss the idea of anyone having mediumship abilities. Of course, just because some charlatans choose to con people, it doesn't remove the authenticity of other, genuine mediums. In the psychiatric and psychological community, there has been some talk and study of mediumship being a form of schizophrenia. However, those who debate for the subject and are pro-mediumship make the argument that the information that comes through is often relevant to *another* and not the individual passing along the information.

Séances

Of course the topic of mediumship wouldn't be complete without speaking to the topic of séances. *Séances*, by definition, are a group of people, usually sitting around a table, hoping to communicate with the other side. Much like table tipping, séances became widely popular in the late 19th century. It's widely known that Mary Todd Lincoln, the wife of President Lincoln, was a part of several séance sessions in hopes to gain contact with one of her deceased sons, Willie. Its popularity grew and, over time, became quite "in fashion" to have parties centering on the séance.

Mary Todd Lincoln

There is much debate about spirits crossing over. Sometimes, when you have contact with a spirit, there may be the issue of the soul still being Earthbound not *wanting* to cross over or the spirit may not know it's no longer in the physical body. When that is determined, you may have to make the choice to decide if you, as someone with the ability to communicate, should let the soul know its state and help it cross over to the other side. One school of thought is that the natural state of the soul, once out of the physical body, is to be on the other side with deceased relatives, friends, etc. Another theory is that it should be up to the soul, itself, what state it should be in (whether here on earth or crossed over to the other side) and acknowledging something that it may not want to recognize within itself could be, potentially, upsetting not only for the spirit in question, but also for the people and property around it. If it becomes angry over its state, it may become violent. Either way, the choice is yours. But, I do recommend some consideration over this topic, especially if you are interested in paranormal investigation.

One last thought: Mediumship is the most rewarding work that I do. Being able to connect a mother with her lost child or a husband with his wife on the other side is the most wonderful feeling in the world. Bringing these people closer to their faith that the soul still exists, communicates, and *loves* is the most beautiful gift, and I'm honored to be a part of the connection. I love all the work that I do (I can't stress that enough), but being able to allow loved ones to know, beyond a shadow of a doubt, that all is well on the other side can heal so deeply.

Auras

Auras ARE THE ENERGETIC fields around the body (and any living, growing creature) that radiates colors and change shape with every thought, feeling, and breath that the body has. I'm fortunate to be able to see these fields around people, animals, and plants. It's suggested that the purpose of the aura is to somewhat buffer our physical body from unseen, invisible etheric energies. Although some clairvoyants claim to see and read the aura, there is no scientific proof that it actually exists. It's believed that we are not born with an aura. It's theorized that our aura develops over time, building in intensity and size with all of our experiences.

Auras are often perceived with colors that typically mix in and out. Think of a swirled Easter egg. It's uncommon to hear of an individual having only one color in her aura. Also, it's rare for someone to consistently only have one "type" (size and shape) of aura as well. As I mentioned, our aura can and does change with all things that affect us. Whether it is a health issue/concern or a new romance, our aura will reflect it. As such, if an individual is able to psychically perceive the aura, it can be read as colors and shapes denoting different feelings and situations. Let's talk about some (by no means is this comprehensive) of the meanings of the colors of the aura.

Bobby Sullivan and his aura.

Red

Red signifies passion, but not necessarily in the romantic way. Red in the aura speaks to a person of great passion *of life.* They have very strong convictions and may be quite stubborn. Often strong leaders, red aura'd people have a strong sense of goal and achievement. They frequently know exactly what they want to accomplish and how to get there.

Orange

Those with a predominance of orange in the aura have an extreme side to them. It doesn't mean that they react extremely, but they often want to go above and beyond limitations. These are the folks who look to take sports or any other competition to the next level. They don't just want to ski down the mountain; they want to jump out of a helicopter, parachute in, *and then* ski down.

Yellow

I always think of those with a lot of yellow in their aura as life's cheerleaders. They are regularly cheery and want to celebrate everyone's accomplishments. Overall, they seem to have a great deal of happiness; however, it's these people who sometimes let their own needs be forgotten as they are busy encouraging everyone else.

Green

Those with a great deal of green in their aura are natural healers. They don't necessarily feel the need to pursue their MD or PhD; however, they emanate healing vibrations. They seem to find random, unknown people approaching them telling them about their problems. Albeit not everyone can *see* an aura, it's common for someone to at least perceive it, even if it is subconscious. "Greens" need to remember to take care of themselves and remain balanced and centered.

Blue

Blue is a rather unusual color to see in the aura. As we are so busy in our day-to-day lives, we rarely find time for peace, calm, and serenity, and that is what blue signifies in the aura. It's believed by some psychics that there are children, coming to Earth now, who have a great deal of blue in their aura. These children are called "indigo children" due to the deep, ocean blue that is perceived in the aura. These children are said to have a high psychic predisposition and are looking to bring the world's population to a new spiritual level. More on this in Chapter 10.

Violet

Blue is unusual to see in the aura, but violet (or purple) is more uncommon. A violet aura speaks to a person of heightened spiritual awareness and enlightenment. Spirituality is a key factor in people who have violet in their aura. They have let go of their egos and allow the universe and spirit to guide them in all aspects of their life. However evolved they may be, those with violet in their aura need to be conscious of not becoming overwhelmed with the trials of pain and suffering that occur on a worldwide level.

Pink

I had to mention pink for several reasons, but most of all, I see it around those who are in new relationships and it makes my heart sing. As you can guess, having pink in an aura is all about love. Especially new love. In addition, pink signifies a selflessness that an individual has. Pink, unfortunately, is not a color that I see residing in auras frequently. It will be there for a bit, but as events transpire, it transforms into other colors.

Again, this is not an all-inclusive list of colors that you will find in an aura. As a matter of fact, if you perceive an aura, you'll typically see several colors. If the colors are generally true and vibrant, the individual is in good health and aware of their situation(s). However, if you find that you see the colors as being muddy or faint, that could be a sign of an illness or unhappiness. For instance, a grayish-green color could speak to someone not feeling well. Or a dirty red could mean lack of clarity.

Just like the colors, shapes can also assist defining an aura. Shapes can vary from circular to sharp, multisided, and edgy. A "typical" aura almost looks egg shaped with the "point" of the egg over the crown of the head. But, working in the psychic world, you'll find that nothing is typical! A jagged shaped aura typically speaks to someone who is fighting within himself. There may be anger directed at another person or perhaps at a situation; however, he is internalizing it for whatever reason. In addition to the shape, you may find that you can sense the "flow" in the aura. If you see colors and the shape moving freely, that, again, speaks to a well-balanced individual. If you notice that the energy *isn't* moving, the person may be "stuck" in his situation unable to find a solution or free himself from it.

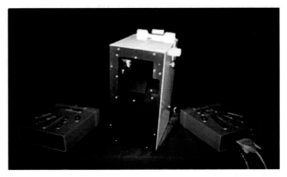

An aura camera owned by Bobby Sullivan.
www.bobbyosullivan.com

A discussion on auras must include the concept behind Kirlian photography. In 1937, Semyon Kirlian discovered that he could photograph what he perceived to be the aura around objects. By placing an object on photographic film (the "stuff" that they make negatives out of) then taking a photo, he found that a halo-like glow would appear in the picture. He felt that this halo was the energy around the object. Currently, there are various "aura cameras" somewhat based on Kirlian photography that have sitters place their hands on electrodes and in turn receive a picture of themselves with colors around them.

Chakras

THE WORD *chakra* IS DERIVED from the Sanskrit word for "wheel." As applied to metaphysics and psychic development, our chakras are the "wheels" of energy that are part of our etheric body. These "wheels" are, actually, the point(s) of entry filling our aura. There are seven major chakras, but several minor chakras within the entire body. I think of it this way: Anywhere you have a joint and can bend, there is a minor chakra. These energy points are often perceived as circular and stationary, but rotating (as if on an axis) clockwise in a healthy body.

The seven major chakras span from the base of the spine to just over the crown (top) of the head. Each chakra aligns itself with different physical characteristics and parts of the body as well as spiritual growth and development. In addition, each has a color that is associated with it. As the chakras are based on Hindu philosophy, the chakras have Western- and Hindu-derived names. Taking time to focus on each chakra, even if it's only the color of the chakra, will allow you to connect with it and keep it open and balanced. Let's look at the major chakras now.

Root Chakra/Muladhara

The root chakra is connected to the base of the spine. It's energetically related to familial issues (sometimes called the "clan" chakra), basic necessities such as food, shelter, etc., as well as sexuality. In regards to the physical body, it works with our physical strength and our basic senses. It's perceived as a deep red color and is often connected to the stones garnet and ruby. Kundalini energy (coiled energy often shown in a likeness to a serpent at the base of the spine) is also based in the root chakra.

Sacral Chakra/Svadisthana

This chakra is centered in the lower torso area. This chakra is often seen as orange in color (I often see it as the bright orange of the sun at sunset) and its energies are connected to relationships, reproduction, and emotional needs.

In the physical body, it corresponds to the reproductive system. This chakra is said to give you a boost of energy in a panic or crisis situation. If this chakra is in dysfunction, you may have an overwhelming sense of guilt.

Solar Plexus Chakra/Manipura

The solar plexus chakra is often seen as the color yellow and is located right above the navel below the breastbone. It is thought that this is the seat of intuition and where we receive our "gut" instincts. In addition, it also speaks to the issues of ambition, career change, and personal power. In the physical body, it is related to digestion and the pancreas. It is also said that the ego is housed in the solar plexus chakra, giving us information on our place in the world.

Heart Chakra/Anahata

The heart chakra is exactly that, the chakra placed right over the middle of the chest in the heart region. And, as you would probably guess, this chakra reins over all things related to the heart: Love, romantic relationships, and compassion. This chakra is frequently perceived as green, but sometimes those with the ability to psychically see the chakras feel they see it as pink. In the physical body, the heart chakra governs the circulatory system and breathing. The stones rose quartz and emerald enhance the heart chakra.

Throat Chakra/Visudda

Communication is what rules the throat chakra. As the name implies, this chakra is placed at the top of the throat just under the chin. If you do not choose to express yourself and instead hold things back, this chakra can manifest a sore or a scratchy throat or even laryngitis. It's visualized in a lovely ocean blue and on the physical body, it aligns itself with the thyroid, mouth, teeth, and gums. In addition to self-expression, this chakra is called upon when you need to find truth and integrity.

Third Eye Chakra/Ajna

The third eye chakra is where psychic information enters into the physical body. This chakra is said to have a deep, indigo blue color and is located in the middle of the forehead. Within the physical body, the third eye chakra is connected to the pineal and pituitary glands, which govern sleep. Emotionally, the third eye chakra works on judgment and balance. Blueberries, raspberries, and red wines are reported to help stimulate this energy center.

Crown Chakra/Sahasrara

Connection to divinity is the name of the game with the crown chakra. It is probably *the* most important chakra when working on your spirituality. Often perceived as violet/purple or an iridescent white, this chakra is located just over the crown of the head. Dealing with such topics as inner wisdom, karma, enlightenment, and opening of the spiritual self, this chakra is represented by a lotus flower that has 1,000 petals. It's said that the crown chakra will not "open" (referring to the flower reference) unless all the other chakras are opening and functioning accordingly.

Although there seems to be much information on chakras, science has yet to prove (or disprove) beyond a shadow of doubt that chakras exist. However, the idea of these whirling vortexes of energy and light within the etheric body has been around for centuries. Much of what we know comes from Hindu and Indian cultures, but we also find new information in our own Western culture from practitioners in the present day.

Healing practitioners (i.e., Reiki, acupuncturists, etc.) from many sects believe and recognize the idea of chakras. Chinese medicine doctors believe in the idea of treating meridians (meridians are, in Chinese medicine, channels within the body where energy travels) within the body for many maladies.

Dreams

THE STUDY AND CONTEMPLATION of dreams and the symbols within have been analyzed by everyone from the ancient Celts to Carl Jung. From dreams that attempt to work us through day-to-day problems to the ridiculously "sci-fi" (those dreams, for instance, that have us acting as super heroes), the world of dreaming is vast. Dream interpretation is a study that is intriguing, at best, and at worst, quite frustrating. It is, within each of us, to interpret all of our own dreams, personally. Although there are several dream "types," all dreams have personal meaning to us individually and therefore all meanings are personal to us.

Carl Jung

Dreams are, ultimately, the manifestation of our subconscious mind—whatever you believe the subconscious mind to be. Some believe that dreaming is really connecting with the divine, with the opportunity to leave the physical body and explore alternate dimensions. Whatever you believe about dreaming, we know that people spend about 25 years of their lives asleep. And in those 25 years, we can experience hundreds of thousands of dreams, although we may not remember them all. It's even thought that babies with their limited experiences dream. In addition, many of us have witnessed our pets moving and making sounds which would indicate their ability to dream as well.

Many people utilize a dream journal to analyze and interpret their dreams. It's well known that even if we don't remember our dreams, we still are dreaming, as it is an integral part of the sleep process. However, for many of us, we only recall our dreams for a few minutes after awakening. Because this is the case, if we hope to assess our dreams and make any sort of sense out of our dreaming, a dream journal is imperative to the process. Dream journaling doesn't have to be complicated or in-depth. Really, all it requires is a small notepad and a pencil or pen. When you wake up, either in the middle of the night or in the morning, do your best to recall what you can about the prior dream. Jot down the details. It may be a bulleted list or it may be more involved, mentioning impressions and feelings. Do whatever is right for you. After a few days, go back and review your notes. Notice if anything has come to fruition that was dreamt.

Remember the thoughts and events of the prior days and see if there is any correlation. What you'll often find, in doing this for several weeks, is that dreams *will* repeat themselves in the same situation. And, you may find that you have written down dreams in the middle of the night that you were unaware of having as you have become accustomed to writing them down. I hear, from many clients, that the habit becomes so ingrained, that they neither remember the dream upon waking nor the notation of it. After a while you will start to see patterns corresponding to events and ultimately, that will be an interpretation in and of itself!

There are various references to dreams and dream interpretation in the Bible. Notice that all of the following verses (and by no means is this an exhaustive list) talk about the interpretation of the dream and what is to come. I think that this is very interesting as many fundamentalist Christians speak to how the Bible is against psychic activity. But, wouldn't precognitive dreams (dreams that allow you to see an outcome of a situation prior to it happening) be psychic activity? You judge for yourself! Here are some relevant passages:

Genesis 41:8: "The next morning, as he (Pharaoh) thought about it, Pharaoh became very concerned as to what the dreams might mean. So he called for all the magicians and wise men of Egypt and told them about his dreams, but not one of them could tell him what they meant."

Genesis (41:12-13): "We told our dreams to a young Hebrew man (Joseph) who was a servant of the captain of the guard. He told us what each of our dreams meant, and everything happened just as he said it would."

Daniel 2: 1-4: "One night during the second year of his reign, Nebuchadnezzar had a dream that disturbed him so much that he couldn't sleep. He called in his magicians; enchanters, sorcerers and astrologers, and he demanded that they tell him what he had dreamed. As they stood before the king, he said, 'I have had a dream that troubles me. Tell me what I dreamed, for I must know what it means.' Then the astrologers answered the king in Aramaic 'Long live the king! Tell us the dream, and we will tell you what it means.'

As I mentioned above, there are different types of dreams. The dreams that we just covered, mentioned in the Bible, speak to *precognitive* or *predictive* dreams. Precognitive dreams are dreams that share, with the dreamer, the future outcome of a past or current situation. However, sometimes precognitive dreams get confused with what are termed *release* dreams. Release dreams are dreams that are often repetitive and seemingly about "possible" occurrences. Their role is to show us how, in a drastic situation, we could/would handle it. Ultimately, they show us our strength. A typical release dream is dreaming of a spouse leaving the other partner. Or a parent losing a child. Both dreams are possible, but extreme. So, there is sometimes confusion about these types of dreams being prophetic, but they are not. Some might classify release dreams as a "nightmare." Another type of dream is what I call a "problem solver." These dreams show us current problems that need to be worked through.

A great example of this is how to rearrange a room. Sometimes, during our dream state, our mind works through tough issues and gives us creative solutions that we didn't see in our waking state. Another type of dream is when our soul actually leaves our body. Some think of these types of dreams as astral travel; personally, I call these dreams "flyers." Put simply, we leave the physical body and "fly" out and about. Whether we go to another location in the physical world or perhaps re-visit the other side, either way, we're reconnecting to spirit. Oftentimes in these dreams, we come back with information that relates to our life path. There is one other type of dream, and it's probably the most common. *Play* dreams are those dreams where our subconscious simply winds out. These dreams are those silly, wishful dreams where we meet celebrities. Or, perhaps we're in the dream state, experiencing something we're contemplating such as a pregnancy. Maybe we're having a perfect golf game… Whatever it is our mind is working creatively to expand our consciousness and show us what is possible.

Astral Projection

Astral projection (also known as astral travel) is the ability to project your consciousness (some believe that the soul actually leaves the body) elsewhere in the universe. Of course, the idea of astral travel relies on the belief that the conscious can be separated from the physical body. Oftentimes, during astral projection, people describe floating above their bodies and seeing their bodies at rest. It seems, as the body is at rest, it is easiest to project. With astral projection, individuals seem to always remember where they have traveled. However, it's common not to know or understand how they left their body.

Remote viewing is another form of astral travel. The expression was coined in the 1970s mainly due to the studies put forth by American physicists utilizing "psychic spies" during the Cold War. These remote viewers had the ability to voluntarily project (some had natural abilities, others were trained) to places suggested by those facilitating the project. Studies were done by Princeton University, the Stanford Research Institute, and probably, most notably, the Stargate project developed by the United States military. Stargate, as well as other projects code named Sun Streak and Center Lane, were mainly in response to the programs put into operation by the USSR. These programs were funded until 1995 at which point funding ceased. Of course, remote viewing still occurs today. Various organizations use remote viewers for finding lost persons or stolen articles.

Yet another form of astral travel is *bilocation*—when a person is physically known to be in one area and, through astral travel, projects himself into another location where he is seen and sometimes heard. A *doppelganger* is another form of bilocation; however, the pretense of it is somewhat sinister. In an experience of a doppelganger, a person sees himself but in no way could it be a reflection. (Perhaps you see yourself walking down the street.) These omens are said to be bringers of bad luck. Abraham Lincoln was noted as seeing his doppelganger prior to his passing.

I have had the experience of bilocation; however, it was unknown to me until reported by a friend. This friend contacted me and asked if I had been in the Atlanta area recently. (Being from Minnesota, I don't frequent the area.) I said no and didn't think much about it until seeing him several months later. When we spoke, he told me he was running an errand and, giving me specific details about what I was wearing, said I walked by him and said hello. He was so thrown off by the thought, he just passed me, exchanging pleasantries and then moved on with his day. When I asked him to describe the dress, he described a dress that I had purchased two months earlier, but had never worn. However, I had it with me when we were discussing the event. I brought it out and sure enough, it was the exact same dress he had described and seen me in.

Many people, when astral traveling, perceive what is called the "silver cord." Interestingly enough, the Bible makes a mention of the silver cord in Ecclesiastes 12: 6-7: "Remember him—before the silver cord is severed, or the golden bowl is broken; before the pitcher is shattered at the spring, or the wheel broken at the well, and the dust returns to the ground it came from, and the spirit returns to God who gave it." This cord is considered the connection between the consciousness/soul to the physical body during astral travel. Many believe that this cord is the way that the body and the soul reconnect. Because of this cord, many think that this is the natural protection during astral travel—that you will never "lose" your body. In addition to astral travel, those who have encountered a near-death experience have reported seeing a silver cord attached to the physical body.

One major, defining nuance of astral projection is the awareness and the memory of what has transpired and where the soul has traveled. Whether involuntary astral projection or practiced and done with intent, the individual remembers the experience. This is a distinct difference between astral projection and dreaming. Whether traveling to a location near to the body, familiar to the individual, or completely unknown, the traveler knows what is going on.

I have experienced astral travel; however, it was completely spontaneous. My senior year in high school, while sitting in Spanish class, I instantaneously was at my then boyfriend's place of employment. Honestly, there was no intention of going there nor was I connected to the location, but that is where, apparently, my soul chose to go. Before I knew it, I was back in class, in my body. Speaking to my boyfriend later that evening, I was able to relay two of the conversations that took place, as well as what a co-worker was wearing.

As I just mentioned, the location may be quite known, but random and not consciously chosen or it may be quite directed and focused. As mentioned, remote viewing is done with a particular place and time in mind; however, that kind of directive usually takes quite a bit of skill and practice. Spontaneous projection, albeit interesting and compelling, can be, at first, quite disorienting however familiar the location may be. Those who experience astral projection either spontaneously or voluntarily report that on occasion they hear a "pop" when leaving the physical body. It's likened to pushing air out of a container.

Many believe that if we perceive ourselves to be flying in a dream, we have actually left our bodies and are in astral projection. Now, this leaves a fine line between dreaming and astral travel, but, what we find in those dreams of flying is that you often hear the participant state that it "was so real." They will tell you that they felt the wind, dips, and turns as they maneuvered and frequently, they were "flying" over a very well-known location.

Meditation

Meditation IS THE ART OF STILLING and calming the mind in the hopes of gaining divine insight, enlightenment, or ascension. Make no mistake; it takes great discipline and focus for meditation. It's not something easily done. However still you may keep the physical body, the mental aspect of an individual is difficult to quiet and relax. Meditation has been practiced within, alongside of, and outside of religion. Not only is it part of various religious doctrines, but it has now also become a therapeutic way of dealing with the hustle and bustle of everyday life.

There are various types of meditation, but they simplistically can be broken down into two: guided meditation and still meditation. *Guided meditation* is one where a voice (live or recorded) leads you toward images, emotions, etc. to produce a state of relaxation. This voice allows the mind to focus on specific points directed by the leader, not leaving room for random thought. For those who struggle to calm and silence the mind, this is a wonderful option. There are many recordings (CD, tape, mp3) available for purchase at book, retail, and online stores.

A sand meditation garden.

A specific form of guided meditation is called *transcendental meditation*. Coined and trade-marked in the 1960s by guru Maharishi Mahesh Yogi, transcendental meditation allowed the person meditating to repeat a word or a mantra over and over, chanting to create a euphoric and blissful state. This was done each day for 20 minutes with the eyes closed sitting cross-legged. "Om" was a common sound used, as it was believed that this was the sound echoing as the world was being created. However, any sound that you feel familiar with and that is calming can be used. Various research and studies have been done on "TM" (as it is often referred to) and it's been found to be quite healing for bronchial issues, sleep disorders, and blood pressure. We'll talk more about the health benefits of meditation in a moment.

Alternatively, *still meditation* (otherwise known as *quiet meditation*) is just what it says. You work in solitary to quiet the mind and let yourself relax into a state of nothingness, ultimately opening but clearing the mind. Often, this can be achieved by simply "following the breath." In other words, maintaining deep and steady breathing allowing the inhale and the exhale to be the same length. What is wonderful about this form of meditation is that it can be performed anywhere… in public or private.

Although there are types of meditation, there are no rules. Meditation can be performed standing, sitting, walking, jogging, or even lying down. Feel free to try different things to discover what works best for you. I often suggest to clients to do this form of meditation just before getting out of bed in the morning as a psychic development exercise. You'll often get information on what is to come in your day ahead.

Remember, clearing the mind with meditation helps open up your psychic abilities. Simply, opening the mind clears the consciousness to be able to hear, see, feel, and observe psychic information as it needs to come through. If the mind is cluttered with stress, tension, or details from the day to day, there is little knowledge that can be obtained.

The history of meditation is one that is as old as life itself. It's been documented that meditation has been practiced for over 5,000 years in different forms. All the true masters of all the world's great religions (the historical Buddha under the Bodhi tree; saying the rosary in Catholicism; Muhammad, the prophet in the Islamic faith was reported to meditate in long, sustained periods) practiced and spoke the benefits of meditation. The Bible speaks of meditation in various places including Deuteronomy 30:1 and Joshua 1:8.

As I mentioned, it's well known that there are various health benefits associated with all forms of meditation, one being the slowing of the heart rate. This assists with blood pressure and overall stress of ordinary life. Another is the oxygenating of the blood. This allows your body's internal organs to process more efficiently. It's recognized by the medical community that if you have enough oxygen in your body, it's almost impossible to become ill. In addition, meditation can contribute to pain reduction, focus, and concentration, and boosting the immune system. Overall, this is a very easy, economical way to maintain health and well-being!

Meditation is frequently linked to other modalities and studies. Yoga and meditation are commonly linked because yoga uses some meditation techniques (particularly the focus on breath) within the practice. Just as in meditation, in yoga you become more aware of your posture, breathing style, and balance. Many metaphysical practitioners link meditation to psychic development and communication of spirit. It is believed that you can connect with the divine source in a more efficient, open way by practicing meditation often. As it clears your mind of your own thoughts, it's believed that you'll open to other forms of communication.

The results of meditation can be as varied as the individuals utilizing this ancient practice. Some find that visions result due to the opening of consciousness. Others find that they are simply calmed and quieted by the peace that a few minutes alone gave them. More still find the art inspiring and take from it a creative boost! Whatever the outcome, it will always be a positive experience! Although difficult at first, the more and more you practice, the quicker and easier it will become to silence your mind. Don't become discouraged. Play around with your personal practice. Find out what works for you!

A long time ago a great sage stated, "praying is talking to God where meditation is listening."

Automatic Writing

Automatic writing (sometimes referred to as spirit writing) is often seen as an extension of clairvoyance and/or channeling; however, the individual writing (or sometimes typing) the material is typically unaware of the process. Sometimes in a trance state, but more often quite awake, those with this ability feel as if words are coming through them, but not of them, as if the words were directed to the hand or the writing utensil itself. They are not communicating their own past history, education, or beliefs, but announcing messages from some other dimension. They, frequently, aren't even aware that it is happening, even when wide-awake. Some believe that a spirit (related to mediumship) directs the messages hoping to pass along communications to their relatives or something that they may need to resolve.

Unfortunately, many people are skeptical of automatic writing. It's been speculated that automatic writing could possibly be an individual picking up, through extra sensory perception (ESP), the thoughts and feelings of those around her. Others believe that automatic writing may just be communicating subliminal information that is within the mind, but not consciously known. Yet another theory is that it's all a fabricated situation and completely false.

Although quite difficult to practice (frequently automatic writing happens spontaneously) there are a few techniques you can use to work on expanding your abilities in this direction. First, make certain that you are in a quiet, peaceful place. I recommend sitting upright and not laying down. As you are trying to relax your mind to connect with divine messages, you don't want to fall asleep. Of course, have a piece of paper (I believe a notebook to be best as you may want to keep your messages compiled) at the ready as well as a pen or pencil. From there, simply allow your mind to clear and try to let the messages flow without you consciously writing anything. Remember that it may be words, pictures, or symbols that come through. Don't try to lead the session in any way that might taint your results. Don't get frustrated if you don't find results right away. It may take quite some time before you receive anything that you can understand and interpret.

Overall, find out what works for you and work to develop that technique. However, remember to give each and every process at least a few attempts. Very few things will work for you on the first try. As with everything, perseverance and consistency are key.

©istockphoto.com/centrill

Helpers

THERE ARE VARIOUS CONSCIOUS SPIRITS that we can ask for assistance on our psychic development journey. I have used, and more importantly, *welcomed* the alternate perspective of these benevolent souls that are willing to work with us, although they reside in a different dimension. Many of us are aware of angels and spirit guides, but there are others such as animal totems, fairies, ascended masters, and the divine consciousness itself. By no means is this list exhaustive. There are many other forms and beings that assist us in day-to-day life. We'll discuss a few of these otherworldly assistants here.

Many people ask how they will know if a spirit is safe to work with and if they can be mislead by a low-level (malevolent) spirit. Unfortunately, it can happen, but it's nearly never the case. Several things happen and warn us if we are aware of them. First of all, your physical body knows when something is not right and not "from the light" (a term we use in the industry to speak to those dark energies that may look to coerce us). You may feel nauseous, achy, etc. Additionally, these types of spirits often want something in return for their information. This is a big "red flag," if you will. If a soul is truly trying to help you, it will want to help you for your benefit to connect with the divine and strengthen your personal faith. Lastly, there is a concept (most often associated with Christianity) called the *gift of discernment*. The gift of discernment is a spiritual ability to be able to distinguish between what is good and what is false. The church says that this "gift" (their term, not mine) is only given to some, but I believe, with heightened awareness, we can all be cautious and know when something is wrong or right. In the next chapter, I'll speak to psychic protection that can also assist with this issue.

Spirit Guides

SPIRIT GUIDES ARE THOSE souls, on the other side, that we have chosen (we may have had a past experience or life with them and they know our goals) to guide us in this current life on Earth. Psychic information oftentimes comes from these helpers. As they are quite aware of what we have chosen to accomplish in the current lifetime, they are looking out for our best interest. However, we always have free will no matter what guidance they may give us. It's believed that our guides helped us create the "chart" that we laid out for ourselves before we incarnated, giving us suggestions on everything from how to work through karmic issues, who our parents would be, where we should place ourselves geographically, etc. As you can see, they are very involved in our Earthly lives from start to finish.

As I mentioned, initially our spirit guides help us to gather ourselves and consider all the things that we want to undertake while in the human body. There isn't one nuance that they aren't aware of in our lives. My clients repeatedly ask me if there comes a time where we could pester them too much. The answer is absolutely no!

Remember this: They signed up (so to speak) for this opportunity to assist you. They aren't going to back out halfway through the job! In addition to, ultimately, planning our incarnation, they also help us through things when we are living the life we set forth. Whenever there is a decision to be made, know that your guide(s) is right there with you gently "whispering" to you the best alternative for whatever you're going through.

Spirit guides communicate messages to us in various ways. As I mentioned above, they do, subtly, "whisper" to us daily. A familiar way to associate a spirit guide to something learned is to think of the Greek story of the "muse." A muse would gently whisper to an artist to help them create beautiful artwork. In the same vein, spirit guides work with us as physical beings. However, we often take in those messages as our own inner dialog. To them, the ultimate goal is for you to receive the message. They don't need the credit. Another way that they communicate is through vibration. How many of us have walked into a room or shaken a hand of someone and felt odd or hesitant immediately?

We know that the reaction isn't from us, as we didn't have any preconceived notions. However, our response was very real. This is our guide(s) working to protect us from harm or unneeded stress. Two other ways that they communicate is through nature and through song. Nature, as it is a purer form of energy, can speak to us as requested by our spirit guides. Have you ever been in turmoil about something and looked up to find your favorite bird right there? Or maybe it's a butterfly… Either way, this is our dear spirit guide letting us know that we are not alone and that they are working on an outcome for us. In the same vein, how many of us, in a bad mood, perhaps from the day's events, hear a song that is a favorite, but it's one you haven't heard for months or years? Well, our guides are letting us know of their love and connection to us.

There are many, many ways that our spirit guides can communicate to us. This is only an example. The bottom line is that they are always at work, for our benefit, trying to let us know the best path in our lives.

My clients and students often ask me if our spirit guides are our relatives. In my experience, the answer 98% of the time, is no. It's not that our relatives don't love us and don't communicate with us on the other side. They do. Quite frequently, as a matter of fact. However, the difference is this: They don't want to influence us in a way that impedes our path and evolution.

Here's my example: My grandfather "Bud" passed away a few years ago. He was a good man, but never really understood my profession. It was never a point of contention, just a generational issue. He would have been much more satisfied if I would have continued my career in marketing or been a dental hygienist, etc. Those are things he understood. However, once he passed over, *had* he become my guide, I probably would have felt very compelled to start looking in someone's mouth. Albeit that we get a greater understanding when we pass over, we still retain our personality and sense of humor. As such, he would have seen a more traditional line of work for me. But that is not my path. So, he is not one of my guides. Has he communicated with me? Yes. But he doesn't involve himself in my career path. All of that being said, does it *sometimes* happen? Yes. But in over 20 years of doing readings, I've only seen a relative as a spirit guide approximately four times. That's it.

You've probably noticed that I've used the word "guide(s)" quite a bit. We typically have more than just one guide working with us at any one time. As we have so much filling up our lives, we need to have a team working with us. Now, I do believe that we have only one "birth guide" that does not transition out of our life. However, it's been my experience that other guides come in and out of our lives with different phases, ages, needs, and relationships. Again, all of our guides are chosen by us and fully aware of what our personal goals are. But, just like the physical world, there are souls on the other side that have specialties and are directed to assist us only for a short period of time.

Many people ask if any soul can become a spirit guide. I believe that any one of us could ultimately become a guide if we so choose. However, you have to remember that when you commit to doing that job, you put aside your own personal evolution to help someone with his or hers. Now, the argument could be made that through your assistance you learn by proxy. However, learning vicariously through another is never the same as having the situation posed to you. Many psychics believe that when you make the choice to become a guide, you have decided that you will not further incarnate. Honestly, I'm not certain one way or another, as I believe so strongly in free will whether you're here on Earth or on the other side.

Angels

WHAT IS AN ANGEL? To many people, angels are many things. However, we need to start from a baseline that we can all take from. So, for the sake of simplicity, let's define an angel as a being from a higher plane (i.e., Heaven) that is supernatural and a messenger of the divine. In fact, the etymology of the word *angel* in Greek means "supernatural being" and in Latin means "messenger." Often depicted with wings, these divine creatures seem to carry out tasks driven by a higher power.

Sometimes perceived as warriors and other times nurturing, angels have a long list of myth and legend associated with them.

Almost every culture in the world has a version of angels. In the Hindu tradition they are known as *deva*. Devatas (the plural of deva) are semi-divine beings that work to serve supreme beings. Much like the demigods in Greek mythology, a deva was said to follow a higher God or Goddess. In Buddhism there are *bodhisattvas.* These souls were highly evolved, enlightened beings that chose not to enter in to Nirvana, but to remain on the Earth to assist others with their evolution and spiritual path. Pagans don't necessarily have angels per say, but they have various Gods and Goddesses, within a hierarchy, ruling over specific causes. In the Shamanistic tradition, we find the aspect of winged creatures (birds such as eagles and crows) providing healing and carrying messages from the Great Spirit to humankind. Judaism, too, has angels as prevalent as the Christian traditions do. In quite the same manner, they are winged beings bringing messages of God.

So what is the difference between a spirit guide and an angel? In my opinion, the answer is quite simple. Angels, being only for the glorification and service of God, do not incarnate into a human body for an entire lifetime. However, they can take human form, for a short period of time, to bring messages, healing, etc. to us, as humans, as directed by the Creator. However, for some, the answer is a bit murkier. Some believe that our "guardian angel" is the same thing as our spirit guide. This may be a semantics issue or a theological one. Ultimately, as with so many other things in the metaphysical world, you will have to determine what feels right and what works well for you, personally. As with so many things around psychism, there is no right and wrong.

©istockphoto.com/Rob Blackburn

Most of us are familiar with the archangels, but not as aware of the other classifications. Late in the 4th century, the Christian church fathers put together a classification of angels and their service to God. Within their hierarchy there are nine types of angels in total, which includes the archangels. Let's look at a few of them:

▶ **Seraphim. They sit closest to the throne of God and are the highest-ranking angels, often depicted with six wings and are sometimes mentioned as the "burning ones." In fact, the Seraphim are the only angels mentioned, in the Bible, to have wings.**

▶ **Cherubim (or cherubs). Ranked just under the Seraphim, Cherubims are perceived to be the record keepers of God. Don't think of these angels as the chubby, winged babies that you may see, as they are quite different. It was one of the Cherubim that held a flaming sword keeping anyone out of the Garden of Eden.**

▶ **Virtues. The Virtues give us the miracles here on Earth. In addition, it's reported that they assist the *Powers* (another type of angel following the Virtues) in keeping the natural world order and the universal laws upheld.**

▶ **Archangels. Probably the most well known, these angels guard the people and material objects of the world. It is the archangels that are most recorded as bringing messages to humankind. It's not recommended that you pray to them for personal reasons, as they are most responsive to communal and societal needs.**

Lastly there are the angels/guardian angels (as named/deemed by the church). These divine beings are the angels that are closest to us as individuals. They will become involved with us personally, if needed.

Some minds ponder if God/Spirit is all knowing and the ultimate creator, why do angels need to exist? I think it's a fair question. One reason is that it is mentioned in the Bible (Exodus 33:20) that no mortal human can see God's face and live. That, of course, hampers the intervention in an individual's life. Beyond this, if God or Spirit were only by itself, it would have nothing/no one to complement it. So, the angels were created for this reason as well. Further it's believed that God, albeit all knowing and all seeing, needs someone or something to carry out orders and the will of God. Furthermore, and probably most important, God deemed it the highest good to create love. As such, God needed a direction for that love and the angels were vessels for that love to be projected to his other creations (humans).

Many people are very interested in communicating with the angels around them. Angels, in my experience, communicate differently from our spirit guides. Their specific callings and designations can be found by research on the internet or various books. I recommend *The Encyclopedia of Angels* by Rosemary Ellen Guiley for further information on angels. Although the methods may be similar between angels and spirit guides, there is a distinct difference between working with each. When I feel angels communicate, I feel almost as if I'm being downloaded with information rather than being told individual facts. In addition, I feel a bit out of my body and light-headed. Angels tend to give information to more than just one person. Frequently they will speak to a number of people in similar situations and give messages that have a great impact on the community. If you are looking to communicate with an angel, simply ask for angelic intervention. It's perfectly okay to request a certain angel for a particular job. But remember that angels are meant for God's work and look at the greatest good. So, if you're looking for something very trivial, you may want to try another route. Frequently the messages are about protection, faith, and soulful guidance rather than predicting future events. If you are looking to communicate with an angel, I recommend doing some research. Find out the angel that is most connected with your need and ask for its assistance. But, remember, it's not your job to pray to them, as they are only helpers in the divine plan.

Animal Totems

A *totem* IS ANY BEING that watches over an individual or group. As such an *animal totem* is one or many specific animal(s) that protect and assist a person or clan. Animal totems are found in Shamanistic cultures all over the world. A little closer to home, Native Americans believed that beyond being a source of nourishment and food, that all animals actually had medicinal/magical powers called "medicine." Bonding with the particular energies produced by these animals could be powerful weapons in healing, peace and war making, hunting, and various other issues that the clan endured. Because of this, tribes associated themselves with certain animals and carried objects related to their totem animal. Whether bone from a deer or a feather from a hawk, the animal totem was a powerful tool.

Animal totems, in a more current capacity, are animal energies that we can relate to and utilize to better ourselves where we may feel that we are lacking. Frequently, those on a spiritual path will carry pouches with aspects of their personal "power animal" (another form of animal totem). For instance, someone may carry a butterfly wing. Or perhaps a small stone carving of a bear. Whatever it is that a person is looking to gain, you can find in nature, in an animal form, and ask those energies to come to you, manifest, and represent themselves in your life.

There are various, common animal themes that people identify with and encourage in their own lives. Again, if you feel that you are weak in an area, look to the animal world to find that energy and draw it toward you. If, for instance, you felt vulnerable, you may want to ask the "turtle" energies to come to you to protect you and create a better boundary system. Here are a few other, quite common animal totems that you may find helpful. As with all of my other examples, this, too, isn't an exhaustive list. As many beings as there are in nature, there are animal totems. Don't disregard insects, reptiles, or sea creatures either. Only a few are listed just for a bit more insight.

©istockphoto.com/centrill

Bear

Of course there are several types of bears, but we'll just talk generally about them here. The bear can bring you courage, as the bear is quite fearless. However, it's believed that working too closely or too much with the bear may bring on a fierceness that is overwhelming in some occasions.

Buffalo

The buffalo represents abundance. Remember that in native cultures, *every* part of the buffalo was used and often, it was central to the tribal survival. Giving its meat for food and its hide for shelter and clothing, this animal was *greatly* respected.

Cat

It's recognized that there are a variety of cats. Big and small. Wild and tame. However, there are many qualities of each that endure throughout. Cats, as a whole, are known to be quite mysterious and associated with magic. If you would like more spontaneity in your life, draw in cat energies. In addition, they are great healers (remember the mythology that cats have nine lives) and will assist you in your own personal healing.

painting by Cindy Kadelski

Crow

In Buddhism the crow is often seen as a teacher to humankind. However, it's also revered to have great communication skills. They have a very broad vocal range to communicate to others in the group letting each bird know its location, situation, and if need be, the predator(s) that may be in the area. In addition, the crow is known for its adaptability. It can be fruitful in all climates and can find food in any and all situations.

Deer

You may want to call on the deer specifically for heightening your clairvoyant and clairaudient gifts. As they have the ability to see in very low light and are very sensitive innately, the deer assist in seeing what is not clearly evident. Also, because of its sensitivity, the deer is a very loving animal allowing its energies to draw love to the individual that uses its medicine.

Dolphin

Dolphins are one of the most social creatures in nature. As such, its energies are wonderful for pulling fun, joy, and playfulness. In addition, much like human beings, family is integral to its social network. So, ask for dolphin energy to assist in family matters. Known for its keen communication skills, dolphins are also helpful when you have something difficult to say to another individual.

Dragonfly

The dragonfly, as many of my clients know, is one of my favorite totems. The dragonfly represents agility, changeability, and adaptability. Because they have such maneuverability, they are able to adjust and make contact with whatever they have set their sights on. Because of this, a dragonfly will assist you in gaining what you feel is difficult or maybe, even, unachievable.

Eagle

The eagle is sacred not only to the United States of America, but to almost all tribal nations. As a beautiful messenger, the eagle transcends both air and Earth being a carrier of divine guidance. Additionally, the eagle will sit, patiently, in a tree for hours at a time, seemingly contemplating its next move. As such, the eagle is a great assistant when it comes to needs of patience.

Hawk

The hawk is my personal totem. I'm fortunate to have a great deal of interaction with hawks here in Minnesota. The hawk, again, in all its varieties, is a messenger—a theme that we see with many species of birds. The hawk, with its keen vision, does its work between the worlds that are seen and unseen. They connect all dimensions and worlds together. However, with the hawk comes strong truth. The hawk will pull apart things that we may not want to discover but need to see nonetheless.

painting by Cindy Kadelski

Horse

The horse, in one word, represents freedom. Bringing to an individual self-empowerment and self-esteem, it's important not to let the horse draw us but for us to lead the horse. Intuitively, the horse energies are leadership, safety, and healing. Horses for many are very cathartic and therapeutic, so remember this if you need someone or something to lean on, but only for a time, as they won't stay in one place for long.

Lion

Lions have the reputation of being fearless. As the "king of the jungle" the lion also represents leadership. A very social creature, it draws in familial energies; however, it can get jealous if something challenges the family structure.

Owl

We find various species of owls all over the world and several are native to the United States. Owls with their abilities to see in extremely low light and with their excellent hearing, can really work between realms. That, in addition to their gift of moving in and out of situations without ever being seen, means this creature is excellent when called upon to develop psychic abilities.

Rabbit

The rabbit, with its gentleness, teaches us to be "soft" in all situations, working to understand every perspective. Also, with its reputation of procreation, the rabbit is a wonderful totem animal to connect with when looking to conceive anything—whether it is a child or a business venture or a creative outlet. One last aspect to work with when asking for the assistance of a rabbit is the skill to see fear. While this may sound odd, remember that if we can see our enemy, we can make an instant change to divert from that path that may, ultimately, put us in combat.

Spider

Within the spider, we can find unity. The spider works to weave its web between two objects, really bringing them together as one. It's said that it was the spider that brought together heaven and Earth. If you are looking to bring two aspects of your life together, ask the spider to join the union.

Exercise

A quick way to work with a totem animal is to carry a picture or stone carving of the animal that you wish to attract. If you're looking for strength, for example, find a picture of a bear. You can print off a picture from the internet or cut something out of a magazine. The representation doesn't need to be ornate. Some people like to find candles that are in the form of what animal they wish to draw closer and burn them focusing their energies on bringing forth the characteristics that are needed.

Wolf

A favorite of many, the wolf appears often in fairytales and in art. Known for its "pack" mentality, the wolf is said to be very social and highly intelligent. What the wolf energy brings to humanity is the idea of balance. Find the balance between work and fun, family, and friends. When that is found, true happiness will occur.

As you can see, animal totems exist to help us through many issues in life. Wherever we may want to better ourselves, we can find an animal energy to assist us in that transition. When looking to discover your personal totem, ask your guides to show it to you. You'll be amazed what you'll find. Often, a pattern of seeing one particular animal (it may be an insect, etc. but I use "animal" as a general term) will come to you over and over. You may see it in the media. You may see it various times on a hike in the woods. However it comes to you, pay attention and trust in what you are connecting with. Over time, your totem may change. Once you discover your current totem, you'll be able to feel and know when things have shifted. At that point, ask again and see what, in your current situation, you are drawing toward you!

Divine Connection

UNFORTUNATELY, A CONNECTION with the divine is not as easily visualized or understood. It's more of a feeling or an opportunity. But, be that as it may, I still thought it worth mentioning. Divine connection is working with the divine within each and every one of us. For some, it's perceived as a heavenly spark, ignited within each of us. For others, it's the universal centering and balance we can achieve in our lives. I like to think of it as a candle, lit by the creator, within the human body in the area of our stomach.

Prayer is often linked to divine connection. I believe, like many others, that prayer is an amazing tool that often doesn't come from us, but works through us. With prayer, just the idea of focusing your thoughts and passing along your issues, thanks, or worries to another, greater, source is so releasing. Prayer, almost by definition, is speaking with a higher (divine) power that you feel connected to. Although, typically, there isn't an immediate return exchange (but it *has* happened), you can feel as if you have done yet another thing in the path to making improvements in your or another's life.

Another way to work with the divine connection is to realize an opportunity when it is given to you. Oftentimes, as human beings, we have situations drop in our laps, so to speak, but we don't know what to do with them. Or, we may not feel like it's on our time schedule to react positively to the occurrence. Because of this, we do nothing, or procrastinate until the situation goes away. You have to remember, along with divine connection goes divine timing—realizing that the divine, in its glorious form, knows the perfect way and the perfect timing for all things. If something happens, so by chance and out of the blue that it's a remarkable occurrence, take note. You have to remember that there really is no synchronicity, only universal timing. Take advantage of every opportunity, put your ego aside, and accept the gift given.

Diving In

A S YOU CAN SEE FROM THE PRIOR CHAPTERS, working on your psychic abilities can be a wonderful blessing, as well as a terrific challenge. Probably one of the greatest hurdles you'll work through is that there isn't a defined way to do/be/believe/learn anything in the realm of psychism. Because of this, you need to become confident in what you believe for yourself. Learning who and what came before you as well as having a good grasp of different definitions will help you build that personal belief system. It will be the foundation for what is to come.

Gaining all that knowledge hopefully has gotten you more and more excited about pursuing the path of developing your personal psychic self. In this chapter, I'll give you insight not so much on background, but what you can expect from the next step(s). From here, we'll explore aspects of psychic protection to what you may receive psychically and how to cope with that information and various things in between. This, my friends, is where you will really turn the corner and address to yourself and the universe what your intentions are.

Protecting Yourself

PSYCHIC PROTECTION IS AN incredibly important topic when learning how to "tune in." It's a wonderful thing to allow yourself to open up to other messages and vibrations, but unfortunately, some alternate messages and energies aren't welcomed nor are they positive. Ultimately, your intention is your greatest tool when working psychically. Just setting the tone that you'll only have positive results and work with "light" (as opposed to dark, and there are those out there who would rather work with that) beings often is all you'll need. However, there are some other things you can do to protect yourself when working in heavier situations. What you need to remember is even though you are protecting yourself, you still will receive psychic information. For some, there has been the fear that if we block certain things, we won't receive information and that is simply not the case.

As I eluded to above, there are those who choose to work with darker energies and beings. Unfortunately, the idea of power and promises made by those negative entities sometimes sounds very promising to those open to their psychic abilities. Something to remember is this: Although those dark beings may promise financial freedom, fame, accolades, etc. it will all be taken away at the height of what you were asking for. That is an absolute. As with all things, only those things that we work for earn us respect and honor in the community. When we take shortcuts there are always severe downfalls.

The first tool that I like to suggest to people is providing psychic protection by using visualizations. There are many exercises that you can find in books specifically written on psychic protection, but here are a couple that I like to use. When taking my morning shower (you can modify this for a bath too), I visualize that any negativity that has attached itself to me is washed down the drain. Therefore, negativity can't build upon anything that is existing. I release any hesitations, aggression, anger, etc. that I may have had from the day(s) prior and let it go. Another form of imagery that I use, especially if I feel threatened in any way (particularly if I'm working on a paranormal investigation), is using my mind's eye and visualizing my entire body encased in what I like to call a "reverse disco ball." What I mean by that is that I see myself in a bubble where there are mirrors reflecting back at me on all sides. So, whatever I put out energetically, I receive back and nothing can permeate this bubble. Lastly, I like to think of this one as the "Shields Up!" visualization. When walking around the mall, getting groceries, browsing at the bookstore or whatever, sometimes we feel, as we become stronger in our psychic abilities, that we're picking up information that is neither asked for nor warranted from those around us. When this happens, I envision a Plexiglas shield (you can have it be whatever clear material you like) coming up, out of the floor, and encasing me. Somewhat like a psychic phone booth. However, in my visualization, I like to leave the top open to allow whatever divine connection is there to remain.

The Power of Prayer

I completely believe in the power of prayer. There isn't any doubt in my mind or body that in any circumstance prayer is an effective tool for whatever warrants it. In the instance of psychic protection, we need to use prayer to set our intention as well as creating boundaries and security for the work that we do. Anytime that you feel threatened in a psychic situation (or, honestly, any other) there are several prayers that you can use. However, wording one right from your heart can be just as effective. Nevertheless, those prayers, such as the "Lord's Prayer" (whether Christian or otherwise), have great effectiveness on low-level energies. The Lord's Prayer has been used, tried, and tested through the centuries. Another prayer that is greatly effective in binding and releasing any negativity is the St. Michael the Archangel prayer.

©istockphoto.com/Duncan Walker

St. Michael the Archangel Prayer

"Saint Michael the Archangel, defend us in battle. Be our protection against the wickedness and snares of the devil. May God rebuke him, we humbly pray; and do Thou, O Prince of the Heavenly Host—by the Divine Power of God—cast into hell, Satan and all the evil spirits, who roam throughout the world seeking the ruin of souls. Amen."

Again, I want to stress that even though this is a Christian (and more specifically Catholic) prayer, it makes no difference as to your faith. These prayers have been used through the centuries and negativity responds to them, as it's a recognizable force of good and faith. There have been several paranormal cases where I have worked and utilized Latin (although I don't speak it), Catholic prayer (although I was born Lutheran), and banishing symbols from various faiths. You have to remember that all of these things have been worked with for hundreds if not thousands of years. They all have strength. Use that momentum in setting your intentions when working psychically. Not only do they have their own protective vibrations, but your belief in them will strengthen their power.

Smudging

Another way of protecting yourself psychically is working with sage and sweet grass and doing what is called *smudging*. Smudging is lighting and burning an herb (most prominently done with those mentioned above) and then utilizing the smoke to create a smoke "bath" to cleanse a person, thing, or area to release negative energies. Commonly, the act of smudging is related to various indigenous cultures; however, the Western culture has similar rituals in its religious ceremonies. Ultimately, the use of smudging creates a spiritual and energetic balance. Smudge "sticks" can be purchased readily online and in various metaphysical and spiritual shops. Some, due to the prominence of sage, pick and bind their own crop to burn in sacred ceremonies.

Smudging clears using the vibrations of the plants/herbs involved as well as clearing the smallest of areas. For example, we could wash our hands over and over, but because water particles are the size that they are, they could not reach into every pore, nook, and cranny. However, because smudging utilizes the air around us, all parts of matter can be reached. So, when we sage our bodies, it's cleansing our skin, but also being taken in and absorbed by our organs *through* our skin. Same with a space. Those walls could be washed over and over, but by using the air/smoke through smudging, it can be absorbed into the walls and space around us. You can find a smudging example on the DVD included with this book.

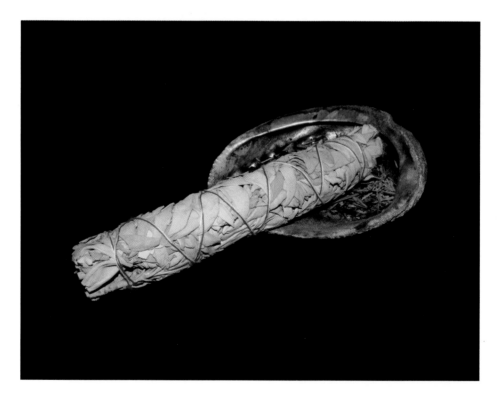

Stones and Crystals

As I mentioned in a prior chapter, stones and crystals have their own energies, some of which work quite well for psychic protection. For protection during a channeling session, I recommend angelite. This lovely light-blue stone draws your angels near to watch over you as you work with the other side, and no undue influence will come into contact with you.

Specifically, with psychic protection you can use amethyst, black obsidian, fluorite, lapis or, one of my personal favorites, seraphinite. Amethyst will work to shield you. Black obsidian will work to repel negative energies. Fluorite will help work against psychic attack. Lapis assists you in opening and remaining connected with only the highest of energies. Seraphinite is another stone that works with communicating with our angels. It allows us to know when and where to act.

©istockphoto.com/Sean Curry

Turning Psychic Info "On" and "Off"

WITH MANY, AS YOU DEVELOP your psychic abilities, you may want to walk around constantly "on." What I mean is being open to psychic information no matter when and where you are. It's something, I believe, that comes from the excitement and opportunity in walking this path. But, as great as that is, I wouldn't necessarily recommend it. Unfortunately, there can be some discouraging and even detrimental consequences to doing that. Walking around wide open ready for any psychic experience can lead to fatigue, over sensitivity, and encouraging negative energies to attach themselves to you.

Tuning in psychically, albeit an infinite energy, is finite within a human body. When someone walks through his day constantly psychically open, health issues, mental issues, and psychic issues can all occur. We can, and all do, handle psychic information coming to us continually for ourselves from our own guides. However, remaining psychically aware to all things around us the majority of the time wears us down. To start, you may have ringing in your ears. Or find yourself with a strong headache. From there, it may evolve into lower back problems or stomach issues (an upset stomach often occurs or feeling constantly hungry). Now, these are just a few of the most common physical manifestations of remaining open for a prolonged time. From there, you can have issues that go beyond the physical into the mental and emotional. I've seen psychics go into deep depressions due to the information that they receive when far too open. They seem to not be able to release what information is flowing *through* them quickly enough and therefore it becomes lodged in their own, personal psyche as if it was their own.

©istockphoto.com/DNY59

Ultimately, you can become drained and your exuberation for development decreases. Feeling drained, psychically, is quite like having a hang-over. Your body, mind, and soul feel as if they're void. But, unlike the typical hangover, you didn't have the alcohol to warrant the feeling. Now, just going through the day-to-day activities can bring this on or it can come on from doing too many readings in a day. Either way, you've exhausted yourself and the only way to gain further information is to recharge and recoup. Sometimes this may take a day. It's unfortunate, but I've also known psychics who have had to take years off from doing readings. Either way, you have to remember that your abilities rely *solely on you* being a healthy, balanced individual.

For some, turning their psychic self on and off comes automatically. For others, it's a conscious decision. I frequently get asked, in completely random situations, if I'm "getting anything" from a location, person, or thing. 100% of the time the answer is "no." Unless I'm being asked or solicited to psychically gain information, I'm just plain old Tiffany. I don't walk around open at all times. Nor do many of my psychic peers. As you can understand from the information above, it isn't beneficial to anyone, neither my clients nor myself. Thankfully, I've developed some techniques to assist in opening up and then "shutting down" or "turning off" my psychic self.

©istockphoto.com/Amanda Rohde

When I first started doing readings professionally, I realized that I needed to create, for my clients and most importantly, *my sanity*, an easy way of opening up. Ultimately, I wanted to tell the universe that I was ready to accept information. However, I wanted to remain grounded enough to be able to pass along the information that I was receiving on behalf of the person requesting it. So, I developed a little ritual. I would sit down with my client, take two deep breaths, and then put a drop of patchouli essential oil on my third eye. At this point, albeit brief (because it needed to be as I was "on the clock"), this was the signal to Spirit that messages could be relayed to me. The patchouli worked to keep the energies (and myself) grounded. Now, you can use/do something similar, or something quite different. But I would recommend as you begin your process that you do find something routine that you can do, in the physical (not just mental) that communicates to the universe that you are ready to receive information. At this point, I don't feel it necessary to continue that ritual; however, I can still feel the shift in myself when I'm open psychically and ready to do psychic work. Maybe your starting point to begin a reading is putting on a specific CD or closing your eyes and taking three deep breaths. It could be holding a certain crystal or stone in your hand to signal, to yourself and the universe, that you are ready to receive psychic information.

Tuning out or turning off psychic information is just as important as being able to turn it on. There are several ways to do this. First, I think it necessary to explain that I believe that psychic ability is never fully "off." I think that it is quite like breathing. It's a necessary part of who we are. So, that being the case, what we need to do, essentially, is turn down the "volume" of the psychic information that comes in. Using that analogy is the first visualization that I use to "tune out." I will see a volume button, just like one on a radio or television remote, and see it decreasing. So, if my psychic opening was at an eight (and it's quite fun to see what your subconscious puts you at every day as far as volume), I see it turning down to a one. Another exercise/ visualization is to see yourself putting on your psychic "overcoat." Visualize putting on some garment that, ultimately, blocks your psychic receptor. Then zip it up. Allowing yourself to be cocooned in a warm cushion of protection.

There will come a time when you may consider the idea of *not* providing a reading for an individual. Unfortunately, some people become heavily reliant if not "addicted" to psychic readings. They look to psychics to tell them what to do with every and all situations. Ultimately, this takes away their own free will. For obvious reasons, this isn't a beneficial relationship. At this point, it is your job, as the psychic, to address the issue. Although the client may understand their reliance, it will be *you* who has to have due diligence and let them find information on their own. Of course, they may become angry. Or they may simply find another psychic. Whatever their response is, you need to keep in mind the best interest for the clients. Additionally, there are times when a client may look to a psychic for a mediumship reading right after the passing of a loved one. I don't believe this to be a good idea as the individual needs to go through her own mourning process before exploring and communicating with the other side. If the person doesn't heal through the mourning process and jumps into communicating with the other side too soon, she will never move through the passing and the wound will continue to be raw.

I can't stress enough how important it is to protect yourself when setting the intention to receive psychic information. Always remember that when opening up, you are letting your body, mind, and soul be used as an antenna for various energies. And all energies are *not* to your benefit. Hence, the idea of protection.

Remember that when utilizing psychic protection in NO way does it block out or discontinue a message that you would otherwise receive. Quite the opposite. It makes those messages of love and light even more present and defined. Use whatever works for you. Although I give you various tips and tools here, what works for you may be vastly different than what I've addressed above. Go with what works for you in *all* things psychic. Just remember what may work for you initially may change over time.

VILLAGE
PSYCHIC

Photo by Tamara

Expectations

THE NAME OF THE GAME, with *all* things in psychic development, is study, study, and more study. What works in one situation may not work on the next. That is why we need to continually keep our minds and souls open to all things psychic while remaining grounded, keeping our ego in check. Previously we have learned about many of the various aspects within psychic development, so now is the time to work with some of those ideas and parameters. Now is the time to set the expectation within yourself that there will be an infinite supply of subject matter and experiences. There should *never* be a moment where you will find yourself complacent in what you have learned and accomplished. There is always so much more being revealed and acknowledged—both by psychics themselves, and also by society as a whole. As much as you may come to understand, you will also find those conclusions becoming new questions to search. Unfortunately, in the psychic world, 2 + 2 may equal 4, but only for a moment in time. From there you will want to know what makes up the first "2." And why do we use the symbol for "4" to represent the answer. There is never a time to rest on your laurels. There is always room to learn and grow.

It may be easiest to set some type of a schedule to work on your psychic development. With our day to day lives, we easily get wrapped up in various activities and seem to put off personal time. Before getting out of bed in the morning, you may want to take a few minutes to simply set your intention to receive psychic information and open your mind to it. From there, you could, on a weekly basis, schedule some time to meditate for an hour. Whether you do this sitting in your home or taking a walk in the woods, this time for yourself to solidify your intentions will work wonders. From there, after a month of working on yourself, you may want to incorporate a friend or peer into your psychic development. Ask this person if, together, you can work to bounce psychic impressions and information off each other. Doing all these things will not only reinforce what you've learned here, but also show the universe your desire to receive psychic information.

Remembering that study is the key to psychic development and heightening awareness, taking one class and/or reading a book does not a psychic make. It's disheartening, but I (and this is honest to God the truth) have seen people take one introductory course in psychic development, then "hang out their shingle," so to speak, and promote themselves as professional psychic readers. To me, that's like taking a CPR course then telling people that you are an emergency medical technician. It just isn't the case. No one is an expert after one attempt at learning. You have to remember that, like anything else, whether it is gymnastics, knitting, or golf, developing your psychic abilities takes time. Don't expect overnight revelations. Although, it's more than likely you will have, on occasion, immediate results in some developmental techniques, it's not going to be the norm.

Study, Study, Study

THERE ARE SO MANY AREAS of psychic study; you could spend the rest of your life in constant, continual study. When you start to explore your psychic self, you find questions within that come forth. Perhaps it's the questioning of your faith. That may be a topic that you need to revisit to reconcile your current path and further define your individual philosophy and theology. You may receive information that changes your viewpoints on society. So you may have to explore alternate ways of living. The areas of study are as infinite as the cosmos. And, as you continue your path, you'll hit, inevitably, on various topics and venture into those that have a draw and stay on the fringe of those that don't.

Unfortunately, developing your psychic abilities isn't as instantaneous as Hollywood may have you believe. Nor does information come through in the ways that are typically portrayed. God bless the film and entertainment industry; I love movies and sitcoms as much as anyone. However, I have never had the experience, nor have I heard of it from my peers, of someone having such a visionary flash that it stops them dead in their tracks. Nor, have I ever heard voices, with my physical ears, giving me psychic information. It makes for wonderful effect and great drama; however, the reality of that actually happening is slim. Even though that is not the typical, or even infrequent situation, it doesn't make the experience of receiving spiritual communication any less impactful or relevant.

Yet another expectation should be the idea of constant scrutiny. Unfortunately, it's human nature to seek out and sometimes judge what you don't understand. For some, this leads to the education process. For others, it means condemnation. If and when you decide to take your studies and development public, you need to know that you *will* be asked about it. Oftentimes questions around your faith will come about. Other times it may be experiences you have had. And sometimes, it's not the questions but the sarcastic comments that are tossed at you. Hopefully this is an opportunity to allow others into your process. It's a great moment to shine. Otherwise, look at the situation as a time to educate those who don't understand. Realize that their hesitation may be from a subpar personal experience. It's easy to make fun of what you don't understand or something that makes an individual uncomfortable.

Remember, while on your path of development, it's best to rid yourself of the ego. It's really exciting when you have an experience where you are validated. The first thing that you want to do is shout it from the rooftops. We all love success. However, remember that for some, your success may impede on their belief systems. Or, they may simply feel awkward about your excitement regarding something that they know very little about. Be considerate. It's a *personal* breakthrough when you have a moment of accomplishment. Unfortunately, in the psychic realm, there sometimes is a feeling of jealousy. You may have succeeded where another didn't and because of this she may feel less than. Of course that isn't the case, but emotions are just that... emotions. If they were reasonable, we'd call them logic!

I have had to deal with a number of situations where people wanted to "test" me or try to prove that I wasn't what I claim. Unfortunately, there isn't a set of rules to go by. What you have to remember is this: It's best not to react at all. And that's a hard pill to swallow. Some people simply want to put others down to make themselves feel superior. You giving them any fight or grief feeds the anger and lack of self-esteem. If you choose not to respond, and remember this comes out of strength, not weakness, you will not "feed" the issue. And, quickly, it will pass. Another suggestion is to educate yourself about various religions and theology. If you can understand their perspective, you will be able to speak intelligently and respond from a place of education rather than emotion.

Another thing to keep in mind and acknowledge is that you may not be able to receive information on everything and anybody. No one is supposed to be, nor expected to be, omnipotent. That would be a contradiction of the divine. We, as humans, are supposed to sit in wonder on many topics. If we didn't, we would never establish faith as a priority in our lives. So, don't worry if you can't "read" something. It may be an issue directly related to you or it may be, simply, that the information needs to come out in its own due time. Don't become discouraged. It's natural, normal, and I can 100% guarantee that it *will* happen at some point.

Lastly, set the expectation that *nothing* is set in stone. You could have all the accuracy in the world, but if someone changes his path or makes a decision that is contradictory to his character, that is his free will. You weren't wrong. But it's not about that. It's about accepting that you did the best you could, passing along the information that you received without ego, and allowing the universe, in its infinite wisdom, to take its course.

Time Investment

WHEN I WAS YOUNG, and beginning my search, I would ask and pray (oftentimes while just walking around the neighborhood) to be given the "gift" of psychic ability. (Again, I don't believe that psychic ability is a gift, but that was what I thought when I was very young, so forgive me for contradicting myself.) I didn't want to be a fashion model. I wasn't hoping to win a beauty pageant or star in a well-celebrated movie. I wanted to be able to connect and communicate with Spirit. That was my one true wish. I would chant it. I would visualize what I would do if given the opportunity to work in that manner. It was within my being. Well, as life progressed, I was fortunate enough to have some amazing experiences that continued my interest as well as my desire for growth in the psychic realm.

As all children do, we phase in and out of things. Particularly in our late teens. But, I always came back to my spiritual roots. In my early twenties, I met and married my husband. Along with finding someone I could share my life with came the reignited passion of the New Age. In a committed, strong relationship, I (probably on a more subconscious level) felt that I could be honest with who and what I was and started, with a new vigor, to study, even further, my interests in the occult, Tarot, psychism, hypnosis, etc. I came back to doing readings for friends and family, although most of them were during a party or social visit to our home. As you can see, my time investment, even before I became a *professional* psychic, was years.

From there, I worked and worked to hone my skill set. I let most everyone in my life know that this was a passion and something that I was not, again, going to let go of or phase out. I began to do readings during the day at my corporate job. Then, out of the blue, I had probably the most mystical encounter of my life during a morning walk with my dog. It was then that I knew that Spirit was telling me that I was on the cusp of a great expansion both personally and psychically. I was physically moved to such an extent that before I even mentioned it to my husband (upon returning to my home), he could see something had been altered within and energetically.

©istockphoto.com/pederk

Following this encounter, I had a further succession of strong psychic experiences that threw me deeper and deeper into my studies. But, then, one day, it just stopped. The information and communication that I was receiving with a voracious appetite just dried up. There was no more. I went from being overwhelmed with the influx of information to absolute quiet. I felt like my right arm had suddenly, without warning, been cut off. It was just awful. Tears of exhaustion (although they were happy tears as I had received what I asked for) changed to tears of sadness. I couldn't understand, with such dedication of both time and soul how this could happen. But I didn't give up. I continued to study and prayed for everything to come back. And it did. And here I sit, several years later, telling you this story.

The moral is to never give up. Never allow yourself the opportunity to quit. Take breaks. Heck, take a brief time out. But don't stop pursuing what can be your greatest success. The time investment is extraordinary, but the rewards are amazing. Not to mention continual. However, you can't expect to give this a try and if nothing is accomplished, give up. This is a journey. Unfortunately, it's not a skill like skiing that you can give a few attempts, figure out if it works for you, and then go from there. The time investment, not to mention the personal investment, needs to be seen and recognized by the universe. The more that you put in to this skill, the more that you will get out. The return will be 1000 fold. That I can promise.

Now, I don't want to discourage you from taking this amazing journey into exploring and deepening your psychic self. That's not my hope or wish. Patience is key. Everything worth having is worth waiting for. I know that I'm sounding cliché, but it's the truth. Part of the time investment is allowing your body to acclimate to the psychic vibrations that will become stronger and stronger as you become more adept. Just like you can become over-caffeinated, you can overwhelm your body with psychic energies and, really, set yourself back.

Overall, just keep a positive attitude and try not to do too much too soon. Learning to take smaller steps with developing your psychic abilities will be, in the long run, of much benefit. It's going to take time, patience, dedication, courage, and perseverance for things to really work when you want them too. But it will happen. Remember, everyone has psychic abilities. However, some dimensions of it will come and work very quickly where others may take years to control and harness.

Dealing with Receiving Tough Psychic Information

RECONCILING INFORMATION, personally, is hard. Each and every day we often work reactively to that kind of data. Sometimes it seems like the world is made up more of the negative than the positive. Of course this isn't the case, but it can get overwhelming. When you make the choice to do psychic work for other people, you need to understand that all that comes through won't be what I like to term "hearts and flowers." That's my way of saying that you will need to see some things that aren't wonderful and all positive. However, there are ways of delivering seemingly less than positive information.

Photo by Evie Haile

I always tell my students that you need to remember to speak to those clients you are working with as if they are family members. You have to detach yourself, somewhat, from the information that you receive; however, remind yourself to be gracious and never, ever cold or sterile. This is their life that you are dealing with and looking into. Despite what you see and what your personal opinions and morals may be, you can never judge, as you have not walked in their shoes. Although you are gaining insight into a piece of their world, you are not omnipotent and don't understand all that brought them to that point. Kindness is the key point in dispensing anything that may bring upheaval to anyone's life.

In doing a reading, you always have to remember to try to see through the negative and look for the reasoning and the ultimate outcome. Unbeknownst to you, the ultimate outcome may FAR outweigh the immediate negative situation. Remember, sometimes it is necessary to lose a battle to win the war. In the same way, sometimes we have to be aware of stumbling blocks on our path to gain great strides later. It's unfortunate, but if we don't have challenges, negativity, and hurdles to jump, we don't appreciate the goodness that comes into our lives. I believe it's simply part of the human condition. Beyond that, sometimes when we are given, seemingly, bad news in a psychic reading, you have to remember that this may be a point where change needs to be made.

And nothing will create change more rapidly than knowing that something that you have planned doesn't go as you thought it would. So, ultimately, the negativity created a positive.

As we receive information psychically, we naturally filter that information through our own personal background and experience. It happens innately. That's why I suggest communicating the information as "raw" as you can. But, nonetheless, we do need that filter to a certain degree just to understand what is hoping to be passed on. Because of this filter and because we are human, we may pass along not only the message, but also our feelings or emotions around it. However, this may be misleading.

The Three Ds

Personally, I will not address certain topics during my readings. I like to classify them as the "Three Ds." This aids in narrowing down any negativity that may come through. Even if the question(s) are asked by my client, I choose not to speak to death, disease, or divorce. I let my clients know of this right up front. First, regarding death, I don't believe that anyone should know the time and place of death. Whether it is his own or a loved one, I think that that is one of the great mysteries of life and should remain that way. In fact, I've asked Spirit not to show me that information. As much as I believe my client shouldn't know that piece, I don't want to be tempted to give that information by being shown time, dates, etc. of death. In addition, I believe that we have some free will around our own passing. I believe that people can let go and cross over due to their own will.

Shortly into a reading for a client, I saw his car falling apart due to it getting hit in a parking lot. Fortunately, no one was hurt, but the car was severely damaged. In fact, I believed it to be totaled. I saw an insurance adjuster standing around the car with my client and handing him papers. Ultimately, I saw this as a bad thing as the vehicle was done and a new one would have to be purchased. However, my client saw this as a GREAT thing as he knew that the car could not be sold for the true value of what is was worth and he had *dreamed* of it getting in an accident (of some sort) where he would be able to get rid of it! So, what I took as a negative situation was, in the end, the best of all situations for him! I projected what I would feel if my car were in the same situation, which wasn't right. I put *his* situation into *my* life and deemed it subpar when in fact it was a true blessing to him.

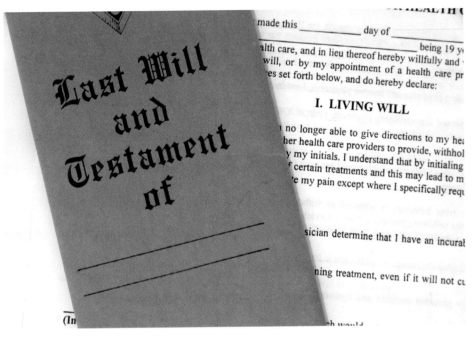

©istockphoto.com/Jeanell Norvell

Secondly, I will not diagnose disease. It's not my place. Western medicine is *made* for that. I'm just a psychic. I don't diagnose. I may see a health issue, but would never, ever take the place of a family medical practitioner. Lastly, within any relationship we have the free will to continue the situation or to remove ourselves from it. So, I won't predict divorce. Certainly, I can look and see if it's in the best interest of my client, but I would never take away someone's free will telling them that they *will* get divorced with absolute certainty. It's unfortunate, but many people continue to remain in poor relationships because of comfort and habit. However, it would never be my place to tell them they must divorce.

Overall, you must remember that anything and everything can change. That's the beauty of psychic information. It maybe be divinely given, but it doesn't take away our ability and opportunity to make changes and redirect our course. As psychics, we need to remember that the first "rule," so to speak, is to be honest. Honest with ourselves and honest with those who trust us to provide information for them. Whatever you receive, remember that is yours only to convey, not to fix, take in, or try to remedy. It's only meant for the person you are working with.

The "Disconnect"

IT'S UNFORTUNATE BUT TRUE. We all, as psychics, will have the feeling of disconnection now and again. The greatest hurdle is to not panic about the situation. It's not as if our hearing or sight is taken away. Although it may be just as wounding. Sometimes, the universe has bigger plans for us that we simply don't understand. In these times it's best to do some personal reflection about what has transpired in our lives to bring us to this point. Take time for yourself. That's what Spirit is giving you. Although the timing may not be ours, trust that everything is as it should be.

When the disconnect happens (and it *will* happen), try to remember that it's okay to not have all the answers. No one is supposed to be or is required to be omnipotent. There will be times, working psychically, that you won't get information you're searching for. Keep in mind that there are *such* blessings to be had in the surprise and spontaneity of a situation. What happens when I run into that situation during a reading is I feel that the psychic "screen" just goes blank. It reminds me of an unused chalkboard. Or a blank paint canvas. There is just nothing there. The "screen" is empty. Now, there is nothing to say that you can't work around the situation by asking different questions or taking a different perspective. However, you may need to accept that you, in the way that you have searched or asked for the information, may not be available.

You may want to try to phrase your intention differently. There is nothing wrong with "pushing the envelope" when working psychically. But, in the same vein, at some point you have to accept the response when you have done everything that you can.

When you have that moment of disconnection, all you can do is be honest about it. You have to be honest with yourself and honest with those who you may be working with psychically. Every psychic that I have ever encountered has readily admitted that there has been a time where they had to dismiss themselves from reading for a single client or pull back from providing readings for a length of time. Usually it's both. Again, remember that we are not meant to provide psychic information for just anyone and everyone. Sometimes it's a matter of the communication style. Other times, it may be that the person seeking information is really not ready to hear it. Either way, you need to trust the process and be upfront about the circumstances.

When I made the decision to provide readings professionally, I worked at a small metaphysical store owned by a woman who had been providing readings for almost 20 years. I dedicated myself to developing a clientele and building my psychic practice. Sometimes I would work 12-14 days in a row taking a day off to do another 12-14 day run. Several months into my reading there, I had a day where I wasn't "feeling" the readings at all. It wasn't that I felt I wasn't getting the correct information, but I didn't feel connected to the communication. It didn't have the ebb and flow of a typical reading. In my concern not only for me, but also for my clients, I mentioned it to the woman who owned the store. What she said to me was quite profound and something I remember to this day. She told me that sometimes, when feeling disconnected *from the information* (not from the divine connection) was when a psychic is most "on." At that point you are putting yourself out of the way, becoming a true conveyance and letting your ego rest to the side. I tell you this story to accentuate a point. There is a great difference between missing the divine connection versus having a disconnect from the information coming forth. Sometimes feeling a disconnect is the greatest form of communication from Spirit.

All things considered, you need to remember that a disconnect from the divine, although quite rattling, is only temporary. Nothing lasts forever, including this situation. Something to consider when it happens is that you may simply need to take a break. In the same way our physical bodies break down through the immune system and create illness to make us all pause, your psychic self may simply need a break. And ultimately, it's going to be for your own good. If you are wearing yourself thin trying to do all you can psychically, you are putting yourself out of balance. When that happens, you simply cannot be of any good (psychically speaking) to anyone or anything. Take rest and relaxation in the moment. Recoup by finding physical things to do with the body. Gardening and knitting are wonderful. And, before you know it, you'll find that your psychic self will be ready, willing, and best of all, *able* to go back to work!

Techniques

IN THIS CHAPTER, I'll share with you some of the techniques I've developed over the course of my studies. As you proceed further and further into your journey, you'll find things that can add to these techniques. That is the blessing of studying psychism. Everything is ever evolving. Nothing should ever remain stagnate. Keep in mind that the information in this chapter is only a sampling of psychic instruction. Nearly every psychic will have tips on how to connect in a different way. I would encourage you to research many different methods and pick and choose what feels right to you. But again, don't limit yourself to only one way as that will only serve to limit your connection to the divine.

Keep in mind, as I've stated previously, that any process may take several attempts for success. Don't become frustrated. Don't fret. You *will* succeed if you just keep at it. I have found, much like riding a bike, a new psychic process may take several attempts, but then all of a sudden you find your "balance" and move forward quite rapidly. Before long, you'll be exploring more and more and deepening your psychic skills beyond your wildest dreams!

Biology of the Brain

IN MY HUMBLE, mostly feeble attempts to explain psychic abilities, I decided to do some research. Bear in mind that I started this research when I was quite young, but I had a lot of questions. I still do. I was pretty certain that I wasn't going to find the answers to "why" some people had a predisposition to psychic abilities, but I thought I might, at a minimum, draw a conclusion or, if I was lucky, form a hypothesis. So, I started studying the biology of the brain. I looked at chemical makeup, research on size, cultural aspects, you name it. I was trying to find out where all this nutty psychic stuff came from.

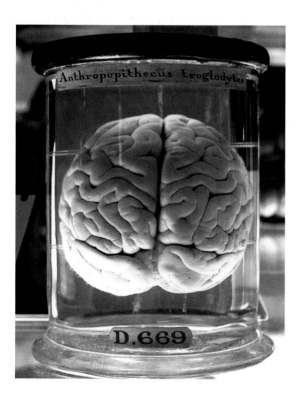

Anthropopithecus troglodytes

D.669

Unfortunately, I didn't come to any conclusions. However, that doesn't mean, even to this day, that I have stopped educating myself. I continue my pursuits. I figure that science will, at some point, figure all this out. Even though I didn't find the answer(s) that I was looking for, I did uncover some pretty neat information. And it *is* information that is useful, particularly in the study of psychic development. It's not a fundamental technique, but it does put some issues to rest that quite readily stand in the way of confidence *around* psychic abilities. The information that I was able to uncover was on how and why the mind creates. And it wasn't just that. I also started to understand how the imagination works. Or rather, how it *doesn't* work.

When working on psychic development with individuals, the most frequently asked question is "How do I know it's not my imagination?" It's a good question. How *do* you know that your mind isn't making up the so-called information that you seem to be pulling out of thin air? Our minds are great expanses of information just waiting to come forth. But, fortunately for us, imagination can very quickly be ruled out when working psychically. This is what I discovered in my studies of the human mind. I didn't find the answers I was looking for, but at least I could eliminate one, pretty significant, potential theory.

Imagination *isn't* psychic ability. But you probably knew that. However, oftentimes, because psychic information seemingly comes out of thin air, we draw the conclusion that it *could* be our imaginations at work. Let me tell you—it's not. I can say this from study, conversations with scientists, and from personal experience. But for now, let's focus on the first two. When I started my studies of the human mind, I found out that we really don't know how the brain creates. There are understandings of the chemical makeup, but the actual process is still a mystery. What we have discovered is this: The human brain really works from what it already has been told, seen, or educated on. Let me explain this further.

The brain is constantly getting bombarded with information. Whether it is day-to-day happenings, training, education, or personal experience, there are a multitude of events providing our minds with new and unique information. Even when we are sitting still, we are continuing our observance of life around us. It's because of this inundation of information that the mind is able to create. Because of the continual expansion, we, even on a subconscious level, naturally expand our imagination. And, our imagination comes from the creative process.

So, if our imagination is part of our creative process and our creative process really stems from things that we have already taken in and assimilated there is *no* way that psychic information can be part of our imagination. Let me use an example to illustrate this point. Let's say that I ask you to imagine. Just imagine. You have to ask me what I'm looking for to conceptualize in your mind's eye. You simply *can't* imagine without something to attach it to. It's that simple. So, I can then tell you to, say, imagine an oak tree and you, in your mind, can imagine that. It may not be what *I'd* imagine as an oak tree, but our ideas would be pretty similar. Because our imagination works from the perspective of what we know or what we've experienced, psychic information can be eliminated from the idea of it being imagined information.

Psychic information is new information to us as psychics. It's not attached to us. It's not information that we have realized in our own lives. It's information, mainly, about others and their set of circumstances. Because of that distinction, we can rule it out as our own "stuff." So, when tuning in, if you get a random name or scenario being played out for you, and you don't find it familiar to you and your own life, wouldn't it suffice to say that it would be actual psychic information rather than your own imagination? Now, if you find that you do in fact have familiarity with the situation, it may or may not be psychic information. Being familiar with information and/or transposing your own set of circumstances in your life to another is something that you'll have to watch out for. Make certain that you are not putting your own feelings, background, or experience in with another. Do a personal check to make sure you're being objective and you'll have great success!

There have been many, many times in many, many readings where a name, location, or term has come through that I have had no personal knowledge of. Most often, it regards a business dealing. Sometimes it's health related. Either way, I don't interpret the information. I spit it out exactly as it's shown to me, no matter how weird or strange I may think or feel the message is. More often than not, it's those pieces of information that are most relevant to the client. The information that you receive that is most distant to you will most often be the most dramatic and important to those you are working with.

Once we come to realize that our imagination has really *nothing* to do with psychic work, it's so much easier for us to become confident in the work that we do. The information received will rarely be yours. In fact, the more adept you get at tuning in and working psychically, the less and less you'll receive about yourself. Psychic work is mainly about the bringing together of a community and a consciousness. Because of this, you'll be able to work much more objectively and with greater satisfaction knowing that you are helping others.

Finding Your "File Cabinet"

I'VE FOUND THAT THE SIMPLEST way of doing things, almost without exception, is the most profound. Maybe that is why after 20 years, I continue to teach the following exercise to my clients and students. It's not hard. In fact, it can often be done in the first attempt. It's a technique that I discovered around the age of 12. This exercise accomplishes one simple thing: To find out where you really are in your mind. It's going to pinpoint where you process information, recall a memory, and draw imagery. From there, you'll be able to identify your psychic information much more readily.

©istockphoto.com/Ed Hidden

This process assists you in determining, once again, what is your own personal "stuff" versus what comes in psychically. And it's not only that. It also allows you to *feel* the difference. Or rather, identify how your own personal information feels. Once that is determined, you then can distinguish between personal thoughts and memories opposed to information coming from the divine.

It's something that is quite easily recognizable, but because we haven't considered the process, we don't think about the method. I've used this technique with children as young as 10 and adults as old as 87. It's been very successful no matter what the age, class, gender, or race.

Exercise

The best way to work this exercise is to have someone working with you. But, it's not entirely necessary. You can even use a tape recorder to give the "illusion" of working with another. What you're going to do is simply have several easy questions posed to you and you are going to focus on and truly *feel* where the information is being drawn from. Often, we don't pay attention to the physicality of drawing information, but there really is a feeling to opening the mind and accessing what we have in there. As questions are posed to you, either by asking yourself, via a tape recorder or with another, you will attempt (and succeed!) to recognize (feel) where your "file cabinet" of information lies. I use the term "file cabinet" as a metaphor for where your experiences, background, education, etc. is found within you. For some, you'll find that it may come from a place near the crown of your head. For others, you may feel that it comes from the back of your head, near the beginning of your neck. And, for others still, you'll find it comes from somewhere totally unique to you. There is no right or wrong location. But, typically, you'll notice that it will come from somewhere around your head and you'll more than likely feel it being drawn from that location and almost pulled to the region of your mouth as if to speak the answer.

A couple things to remember: First, you don't want to use complex questions. When I'm working with my students, I make certain to ask things that are *very* basic that everyone can relate to. I'm neither posing an algebra equation nor asking anyone to relay a word in a different language. As you want to really accentuate the placement of the information, you don't want to spend too much time just trying to remember the answer. So, use questions or statements such as:

"What month were you born?"

"What is your mother's name?"

"Imagine a fire truck."

Those are the types of things that you want to ask. It's basic information, but this isn't a school quiz. We're working to identify location not win an academic award.

Secondly, remember that even though this is a very simple exercise in concept, sometimes things don't work the first time. You may *not* feel the information being drawn or you may feel that it's being pulled from several different locations. Don't worry about it. Give it some time (hours or a day or two) and try again. I've never felt that this exercise didn't work, even if it took a few attempts. There is no need to panic and honestly, if you do, it may hamper your development. Always keep in mind that so much with psychic development is keeping your mind open and being as fearless as possible. There never, *ever* is any failure, just future attempts at success.

As I stated earlier, you are identifying the area of your mind/being where you house information that is pertinent to you. It's those memories, education, and experiences that *are yours*. However, if information were to "come in," so to speak, from a different area, you could conclude that the information was not yours and therefore psychically drawn/given to you. Another way of saying it is if the information is not yours, but it's relevant and validated by an alternate source as its individual experience, it must be from beyond you. Because of this, if information is received from another location other than your "file cabinet," it's psychic information.

This exercise is important and you can really use this as the building block for all future psychic development exercises. If you can differentiate your personal information from what is being received psychically, a whole new world opens up for you to explore. And honestly, having that opportunity to actually *feel* where personal information is being drawn from opposed to having received it psychically (as the psychic information won't come from your "file cabinet") is a great boost to your confidence when working on your own psychic development. If at any time there is confusion about what is psychic information versus your personal thoughts (and that may happen from time to time working with someone in a similar circumstance as your own), you can go back to this exercise, identify where the information was pulled from, and move forward from there!

Sign Work

SIGN WORK IS, in its simplest form, asking for signs from the universe or God to gain information or direction about a certain topic. Signs have been given in multiple, historically recorded situations. From the biblical signs reported to be the prophesy of the apocalypse to the idea that the ancient Mayan calendar stops at 2012, signs are all around us at all times. One of the most common themes and occurrences that I hear from my clients regarding their loved ones that have passed over are symbols and signs that have been communicated to them. Whether it is a butterfly that they held dear or a familiar song being played on the radio, signs are meant to give us comfort and connection when we otherwise feel disconnected.

Using signs to guide us is a distinct process unto itself. Although dream interpretation is a wonderful way of gaining insight, it does differ from sign work. Of course, the most obvious of differences would be that in dream work we are sleeping. In addition, quite frequently in our dreams the symbols given run to extremes. Oftentimes within the dream a sign may be quite vague (sometimes showing a representation of a being) or very direct (showing the actual events in linear time). Sign work lies more in the middle of psychic communication. The benefits of using sign work in our waking, every day moments is that we have much more control, and can guide the information to what we need.

Before I go on, I'd like to cover some common items that we can ask for when working with signs. The interpretations that I include are how I have interpreted and used these symbols. Although they are my personal opinions, there is a general consensus around the symbology of each and I suggest that, if you feel led, you do your own research and determine what each means for you. Remember that they may automatically show up around us or we may specifically ask for them to occur. As I mentioned before with other information I have provided, by no means is this list exhaustive. The signs provided to us by Spirit are as endless as the imagination. Here are just a few:

Water

The sign of water often speaks to what lies ahead. If you are frequently seeing pictures or symbols of water in your life, you can know that you are on the cusp of a big transition in your life.

Sky

The sky is a symbol of transcendence. Working your way through something in the soul—typically, a positive sign of things opening up and gaining ground. Also could be a symbol of creation.

Fog

Fog oftentimes speaks to corruption or manipulation. Someone is not allowing you to see what needs to be seen. And, sometimes, it may be that you are avoiding the obvious. Either way, take time to reexamine things in your life that you may not necessarily want to deal with.

Forest

Forests or a grouping of trees speak to mysticism and magic. Having the symbolism of a forest repeat itself is a sign that there are unseen forces at work, which are typically positive. However, the recognition isn't important, it's the underlying work that is the focus.

Red Rose

It's probably not a surprise that the red rose is a sign of everlasting love. Not only does it mean romantic love, but also the purity of familial love and remembrance.

Shark

Although in some cultures sharks are revered and seen as a sign of strength, our culture seems to have a different take. Sharks frequently represent being overtaken and a fight or conflict that is on the horizon.

Dragonfly

The dragonfly is a symbol of spirituality and personal growth. Oftentimes, this sign comes to us after a hardship to show that we have weathered the most trying of times.

Owl

Intelligence, thoughtfulness, and education are all representative of the owl. This sign typically appears when we are studying a new path that will, ultimately, serve us well.

Feather

The feather speaks to us about remaining flexible and embracing change. Although the feather is soft, it goes to great heights while remaining versatile and vulnerable.

Horseshoe

The horseshoe is an everlasting symbol of luck. However, notice that the lucky horseshoe is always turned up to retain and hold that luck. If you find that you are seeing horseshoes facing downward (an upside down "U"), know that your luck may have run out!

Star

The star is an ancient symbol going back to pagan times offering protection and warding off evil. Even today, law enforcement embraces this sign, frequently wearing badges in the shape of a five-pointed star.

Ancient Pyramids

Pyramids draw our eyes upwards to the heavens. And, ultimately, the pyramid sign reminds us of our connection to the divine. When you find yourself given the sign of a pyramid, remember to further your connection with Spirit in whatever form you may.

Now that you know what some general signs mean, it's time for *you* to learn a specific technique utilizing signs that you may like or prefer. So many times when individuals are looking for a sign, they leave it up to the universe to deliver a message to them. However, as we are all human, and we naturally look to rationalize everything around us, the messages may come and go unrecognized or disregarded. This technique takes that questioning away. It gives you more control over the process and as *you* are picking the sign, *you* can watch for it with knowingness and confidence that you'll gain insight directed by and only known to you!

Exercise

Here's how the technique works. First, select your personal sign for information. This sign can change for each attempt, but for now, determine what you'd like to see and recognize in this situation. You can make it as extravagant or mundane as you'd like. By all means, you can use something that resonates with you from the list above, but don't limit yourself. Maybe you pick your favorite flower. Or perhaps it is something out of the ordinary such as a hot air balloon or a unique species of tree. Whatever it is, I recommend that for your first time, it's something visual. Later on, as you become more familiar with this practice, you can use a song or ask that someone contact you. From here, determine a period of time that you are giving the universe to show you this visual symbol. It may be 24 hours or two weeks. I suggest that you don't give *less* time than 24 hours, but I understand that sometimes we need to know things in a bit of a hurry. Now that you have determined your sign and the length of time to be shown it, you need to make a statement of what you'd like that sign to tell you. You may be looking to find out if it's in your best interest to buy a new car. Or, if the new romantic relationship that you are in is the person you'll eventually marry. Whatever it is, be precise about your question. And, be certain to make it a yes or no statement. I highly recommend that you write down your question to remember how you worded it when and if you receive your sign.

So, as an example of this technique, you may find yourself asking something similar to: "Please show me a red balloon within 24 hours if I should buy a new car." You can see that you are placing all the pieces from above into one, succinct statement, and being quite direct with your request to Spirit. Now, don't fret about not seeing the sign. I have found, when using this process, that the universe realizes that we are not the most observant of creatures. If it's meant to be, you'll see your sign many, many times in the time allotment requested. However, if you *do not* see your sign, that's very important information as well. This, of course, means the opposite of what you asked. So, using the example above, if I did not see my red balloon, Spirit is telling me that it is not time to purchase a new car. So, either way, you are connecting with the divine and gaining insight and guidance.

This technique is a beautiful way to connect with the divine in a way that is simple and quite straightforward. What happens, after utilizing this process a few times, is that you actually start to *feel* the connection not only to the information, but how it also comes in and how it's received. Over time, it's very common for my students not to have to use this method at all as they become more and more aware of their connection.

They find that they can simply pose the question, without asking for a sign, and have knowingness almost immediately as to the outcome or answer. Often, I hear from those using this technique that they may feel a physical presence. Either eyes watching them from afar or it may be a warmth at their back. Other times I hear that they just feel very compelled and drawn toward an action. Whatever you experience know and recognize that connection!

Connecting with Your Spirit Guides

IN CHAPTER 6 I COVERED what spirit guides are. Now that you understand that piece, I'd like to go more into the idea of "why" and "how" they communicate and work with us. Their connection to us is one of love and acceptance. The last thing they are looking for is to take credit for their assistance or to control our lives. Our bond with them is one of mutual agreement and understanding the goals that we have determined poignant in our lives. Although they work with us prior to incarnation on the ways to those goals, they also are very aware of our free will and how life, sometimes, does get in the way. Because of free will, they assist us working us back on our path.

Before I give you yet another technique on how to communicate with your guides, I'd like to speak to how it feels, so your expectation is set correctly. It's very rare that communication from your spirit guides will utilize your physical senses. You have to remember that they are meant to *guide* you, not outright tell you what to do or boss you around! Subtlety is key for them. When you have a communication, it often feels like your own internal dialogue. The only difference is, it's simply not yours. Typically, the information will come in at the most random of times. You may see a brief picture or moving scene. (And when I say brief, I mean *brief*. It's often just a second or two.) You may feel that words are just popping into your mind. I'll "hear" words, names, or dates that I don't have any connection to. Or it may be a familiar taste.

I'll never forget the moment when I heard from my personal guides that I should write my first book. I wasn't looking to write. Heck, I was vacuuming at the time. The last thing in the world I was looking to do was take on another creative project. However, Spirit had another idea. As I was vacuuming, thinking about the day's activities, I simply heard a very low, deep voice say "Write the book." Although I'm pretty familiar with communication from guides, this message took me by surprise. I looked up (I'm not certain why but it felt right) and said: "I have no idea what you're talking about. I don't want to write." A moment later I heard "It's already written." Again, looking toward the ceiling, I told my guides "I beg to differ. I haven't written a thing." After a pause, I heard "Go to your classes." Now, instantly I knew that this didn't mean that I was supposed to *attend* a class. I knew I was supposed to go to my "class" folder, in my computer, and look there. As I did, I realized that I had written a ton of material for various classes that ultimately, became the text for my book. As you can see, this illustrates the brief message along with a feeling to move toward an action.

Quite frequently, it's a combination of two or more of these things all at once or in rapid succession. Think of it this way; it's like watching a half-hour sitcom in three seconds. Your senses will become flooded.

Although you will get information randomly, there will be many times where you will consciously ask for your guides to assist you in any given situation. It's a wonderful and joyous thing for guides to be utilized in such a fashion! Can you imagine putting in all this hard work and no one ever asking your help directly? It'd be tough! So be confident that your guides enjoy and look forward to you working with them and asking for their insights. A question I'm asked repeatedly by clients is if our spirit guides ever get tired of us asking for assistance. The answer is *always* NO! That is what they are there for and you are their "charge." If you committed and took on a task out of love and respect, wouldn't you want to be asked to utilize your gift to see that commitment through? Of course you would. It's no different for our spirit guides. They want to be put into play and work in our lives here on Earth.

But where do spirit guides get their information? Working and communicating with guides for over 20 years, I've heard a few answers from them. Most often they tell me that because they can see the broader picture of how we are acting currently, other relationships we are engaging, and what path we're moving down, it's mainly perspective. For instance, if you had a helicopter and a friend was asking for information on the best driving route to take to a destination, you could go up in that helicopter, see all the factors (traffic, road construction, etc.), and tell her the best way. The same idea works for your guides; they have a better viewpoint. Beyond the broader perspective, they have the ability to access what many people in the metaphysical world call the "Akashic Records." These records (sometimes referred to as charts) carry all the information, for every soul, from the beginning of time. As such, they can see what was and what needs to be, better guiding you on your journey and understanding potential outcome(s). Lastly, they do have a deeper, broader connection to the divine. They are able to work with other individuals' spirit guides to gather information and pass on to us what is in our best interest.

Exercise

It's important for us to familiarize ourselves with our guides. Just like any other important relationship, we should work to get to know them. Once we build that relationship, it deepens our connection to Spirit and ultimately allows us to deepen our psychic abilities. A great way to "meet" your guides is to take time out of your day and do a little meditation and visualization. Start out relaxing your body. I recommend sitting in a chair for this exercise, as you don't want to drift off and fall asleep. Imagine yourself sitting on a beautiful beach. Or, if the beach doesn't work for you, maybe it's in a forest. Either way, imagine yourself outside, on a sunny day, the perfect temperature, pain free and perfectly at peace. As you are sitting there, feel the sun warm your skin... feel the wind caress your body. You may hear other noises in the background, but they are really of no matter to you. It's simply nature talking to you. At this point, as you sit there all alone, *ask* for your guide to approach you and say hello. And wait. It may take a few moments, but someone will approach. Now, they may be somewhat shrouded in shadow or they may be quite visible. Either way, don't worry about it. As they approach, notice what you can about their height, gender, body shape, etc. When they come up to you, gently ask their name. Once a name is given, thank them for responding to your call and see them walk away. Then, ever so gently, bring yourself out of this meditation and again, thank them for their participation. Once you have gotten to the point of getting a name, feel free to go back to this place and expand upon the conversation. It will be where you and your guides will have your meetings and over time, become quite familiar and easier to find.

"Ask and You Shall Receive"

The simplest of all techniques I can pass along to you is to *ask* your guides to work with you in more direct ways. There is nothing wrong with asking for stronger communication from your guides and angels. If someone wasn't hearing you well, and you weren't consciously aware of it, wouldn't you want him to tell *you?* Of course you would. It would be only natural! So, make it known to Spirit that you really do request a deeper, more profound connection and you'll be surprised with what you start to receive. It really does help the process.

To illustrate that point, let me tell you another personal story. When I was very young, as I mentioned, I began my study into the metaphysical. And more specifically, psychic and psychism. I was fortunate to grow up on a lake and even beyond that, I was always outdoors. And, living in a small community, sometimes I didn't have a playmate, so that made time for introspection and thought. (As much as you can be introspective at 11!) As I would wander through the woods I thought about what it would be like to develop strong psychic skills. I thought about those I could help if I opened up my abilities.

I really saw, in my mind's eye, what I would do with my life if I would be fortunate enough and *diligent* enough to pursue my psychic skills. Over time, communications opened up. My mind opened to signs and signals from the divine that even as a young adult I could understand. And, if you ask from your heart you'll find that Spirit will respond to your request.

Sometimes, when you ask for information, and you receive it, you may find that the information was incorrect. Or, more likely, the information was interpreted incorrectly. Don't let that overwhelm you or discourage you. It happens to all of us. We *are* human and can all make mistakes. Remember that, innately, although we may try to keep the communication and the information we are receiving as pure as possible, we do relate everything to what we know. For instance, if we were to ask Spirit about a friend and her romantic life, we may see her sitting across the table having dinner with another and smiling. Seemingly, we could pass this on to our friend as a good visual. She is out being social, and as shown by the smile, having a good time. However, this could mean that although the friend is out and about, she isn't expanding her social circle to find the romantic interest that she longs for. The person across the table from her may be a family member. Or someone who is hindering her finding a committed relationship. Either way, be open to the possibility of an alternate interpretation.

Another form of communication from your guides may be a little less direct. More often, it's a communication to simply let you know that your spirit guides are present and watching over you. I call it the "twinkle lights." When I first experienced this, it was often in the evening when watching television or simply relaxing. I'd see small, sparkly lights that moved and floated around the room. After blinking several times and rubbing my eyes, they would still be there. As this started to happen more and more frequently (a few times a week), I decided to do more research. Although the phenomena has different names, I did find that this was happening to others exploring their psychic abilities. One day in meditation, I asked my guide what this was and she told me that it was simply a "hello" from the other side. My spirit guides wanted me to know that I was safe and being watched over prior to going to sleep at night.

Another request that you can make to deepen your connection with your guides is for them to communicate in your dream state. Ask them to have an open conversation with you while sleeping. You'll be amazed at what you will learn in those moments of peace. I often get asked how one will know he spoke with his guide. It's a great question, and one that is easily answered. If you felt like you were having a conversation with someone dearly familiar to you, but you didn't necessarily recognize his or her face, it more than likely was your spirit guide. Other telltale signs are if the dream was in color and if you were talking in real-time. Now, if you were jumping around to different scenes, it may be some projection of your psyche and not really your guide. But, if those three criteria (familiarity, color, and real-time conversation) were met, it is more than likely a communication with your guide.

More than anything, in all that you do, setting your intention needs to be paramount. And, making your request to Spirit, asking for help, is the first step in setting your intention. Fortunately, in the great design, our guides are there for us to help us in any way we request, as long as it's law abiding! Remember, as you formulate your requests, really picture yourself receiving what you have asked for. And be specific! The more detailed and focused you are will only help your cause. If you leave things too broad, you may get your request, but it may be handled in a way that isn't optimum for you! Seeing, feeling, and directing any wish works to solidify it to the universe. Not only that, but you are showing Spirit and the energies around your request that you have really thought the situation through. This only serves to make you prepared for the scenario to occur. And being prepared allows you to "hit the ground running" when those psychic abilities continue to open up!

©istockphoto.com/Florea Marius

How to Provide a Reading

NOW THAT YOU HAVE LEARNED some techniques, there may come a time where you want to stretch your wings and do readings for others. There are a lot of things, beside the accuracy of your reading, that you should consider. Something to always remember is that the person you are reading for, no matter how well you know her, is putting herself out there and allowing herself to be vulnerable. That in itself if a tough chore.

So, no matter what the information you receive, be gracious. Always be thankful that the client is there to *assist you* in your growth. Because, it's your combined energies that are working to accomplish a goal.

Something that you do not want to do when meeting with a client is create a situation where you are providing a "hot" reading. A *hot reading* is where you take given or previously known information and use it to guide a reading. It's unfortunate, but some fraudulent so-called "psychics" make their living this way. They look to overhear conversations in public situations, then swoop in making a big impression on an unsuspecting individual. From there they let the person know that they provide readings and hope that the person will come to them for further information. Now, I don't believe that someone who is really, honestly, wanting to develop his or her own psychic abilities would ever consciously do this. However, it's a situation that you want to be aware of. Don't ask too many questions or use personal information to cloud the reading. Of course, as we work and develop our psychic abilities, we often read for friends and family. The best thing to do is to remember to really shield yourself from your personal wants and desires for them. A great way to utilize friends that you feel comfortable with is for your friend or family member to ask about someone in a situation that is unfamiliar to you.

Photo by Tamara

Conversely, you don't want to provide a "cold" reading, either. A *cold reading* is one where the "psychic" doesn't ask questions, but makes statements that are quite broad and general, looking for validation. Oftentimes, those who use cold reading techniques are also reading body language, noticing clothing or jewelry, or studying a manner of speech—all of which are quite telling about an individual, but don't make for a true psychic reading. It's basic human nature to watch someone walk toward you or react to a statement you make, but you cannot be led by these nuances. Really tap in to what you hear from your guides and spirit. Don't go to the obvious. Be courageous and really put yourself out there to what your psychic abilities are showing you.

You may consider providing readings in different manners. I started out providing readings in person through a metaphysical shop in my area. However, my schedule has become so hectic that, outside of events, I only provide phone and email readings currently. And as time progresses, you may want to think of different ways you would like to provide readings to the public. Phone readings are generally structured and scheduled by time. You may want to offer different segments of time to match the needs of those around you looking for a reading. Some psychics offer general 15-minute, 30-minute, and 60-minute readings. Others provide phone readings by type, whether it be channeling, mediumship, Tarot, aura reading, etc., with the length of time all being about the same. You have to do what feels right to you. Don't be concerned about not being face to face with your audience. Remember that the physical body doesn't house psychic energy; it's all around us! Geographic limitations are only limitations to the physical. Spirit doesn't have those limitations.

I frequently get asked if one venue is better or worse than another. The simple answer is "no." If one modality was better than another, I would do it. You have to remember, and often remind the person that you're reading for, that what we are working with is energy. It has nothing to do with a physical presence.

Email readings can be a bit trickier, as you aren't getting the immediate feedback if the information coming through is being placed and validated. However, you will know that you certainly are not providing a hot or cold reading, as the information really has no connection to the physical, other than the email to which you are responding. It's a very pure way of doing a reading. Many of those who have provided email readings in the past have now moved on to providing readings via instant messaging, web cameras, etc. As I stated a moment ago, the mode of reading really is irrelevant because psychics work with energy.

Another alternative reading source is working at a psychic fair, metaphysical expo, or something else of the sort. These events are often held in larger areas and open to the public. If it's your intention to work as a psychic, these events are a great way to gain exposure and really develop a clientele. However, I have a few words of caution. First, remember that you, more than likely, will be working in an area with people simply passing by. This may be an issue of privacy. Know that the bond between the psychic and the client needs to be one of confidence and confidentiality. I'll talk more on the confidentiality later, but for now, keep it in mind if you are considering becoming a vendor at this type of event. Further, you need to protect yourself from all the energies that will be swirling around you at these events. Anxiety and excitement are associated with bigger groups and something that you may pick up on. Sometimes it's very difficult to put all that aside and focus on the individual at hand.

As I mentioned, client confidentiality is second only to the accuracy of the reading that you give. The foremost importance needs to be placed on the information and communication of Spirit, closely followed by the trust of your client that what is being communicated goes no further than the conversation between the two of you. You are going to hear the innermost dealings of an individual. It may be things that the person has never mentioned to another soul. Because of that, nothing can be shared with another without your client's express consent. And, even then, I prefer that the client share the information with the third party. Unless there is express communication of a person doing harm to himself or another, all the information gathered in a session stays with me. Period.

Conveying Negative Information

I often get asked if and how I convey bad or negative information. For some reason there is an idea around that psychics should not and do not speak to bad situations. I don't find that to be terribly moral or in the best interest of my clients. Honesty, with anyone, is always so important. And isn't it the harder things in life that make us stronger? Now, don't get me wrong, there are right ways and wrong ways to convey difficult information. I don't think it's best for anyone to get hit over the head (metaphorically speaking) with anything negative.

Always remember that the person that you are providing the reading for is someone's child. Potentially they are someone's mother, father, sibling, or spouse as well. Treat them the way that you would want to be treated. Even bad news can be given graciously and with kindness. Remember that even seemingly bad news can have a positive effect. So, when given some tough psychic information, make it your goal to find out how to steer away from the negativity or determine the ultimate outcome of this trial or tribulation.

Always remember that more often than not, the information coming through is also, in part, for you. Don't think for one moment that the individual who came to you for a reading is random. It never ceases to amaze me that people will come to me with certain issues that I, either currently or in the recent past, struggle with. Even though that may be the case, don't project your own "stuff" into their lives. Remember, everyone is an individual and the situation is personal to him or her. Remain true to the communication that is coming through because what you did for yourself in a similar situation may not be the most ideal for another.

There, unfortunately, will come a time where you will get negative feedback about a reading that you provided. It happens to all of us. I don't care how famous, accurate, or "tuned in" a psychic is, there are always clients out there who will not connect with a reading that we have given them. In those moments, remember this: You did the best you could and you can't be faulted for that. Another thing to consider is there are people in the world that, no matter how "on" you may be, refuse to believe it and will continue to condemn. There are always reasons, typically unseen to us, for the meeting to have happened. Keep that in mind as well. There is no *doubt* in my mind that you provided *something* to that individual that was worthwhile and good. Even if he is refusing to see it. However, remember to own up to what you could have done better. No reading is perfect. Everything can be improved upon, so deal with the negativity immediately when it's presented, and then release it. You'll be better off for it.

Receiving Payment

One last thing to consider when doing readings is if you will charge for them. Whether it is in barter or in actual cash, the idea for charging for readings is a controversial topic. Some believe that being able to provide readings is a "gift" and that it is immoral to charge a fee. Others believe that time is valuable and justify it by that reason. I work with the two schools of thought. Yes, I believe that psychic abilities are a special skill set and definitely unique. However, I also believe that my time is worth something. Here is my argument: Would someone who had a special aptitude in math and made that a profession feel it was a "gift" and not charge for utilizing that gift? Do authors who have a special knack for writing not charge for their books? Of course they all do. Why would being a psychic be any different? My time is just as valuable. Some individuals make the case of "divinity" being in the psychic realm, but do pastors not get paid to work with the congregation? They most certainly do. So, in no way do I devalue my time nor would I devalue my skill set any differently than any other profession. You have to do what is right and moral for you. Make your own arguments and, ultimately, follow your heart.

This chapter gave you a lot to think and act upon. I know that there is quite a bit to work on and bring into your development. Keep positive!

Don't force yourself into anything that makes you uncomfortable. However, take what works and really delve into it. The more you make attempts the more you're going to feel comfortable, achieve success, and gain confidence in your psychic abilities and ultimately, your readings!

©istockphoto.com/Karl Dolenc

©istockphoto.com/Cristian Ardelean

Other Things to Consider

I KNOW I HAVE GIVEN YOU MORE than a fair share of psychic development information. However, I'm sure you are coming to understand that your studies could be endless. In this chapter, we'll explore a few other aspects to consider when developing your abilities and furthering your studies. I believe that there is nothing more beneficial than knowledge. Because of this, let's take our studies a little bit deeper, looking beyond your personal development and more into what you may run across.

Past Lives

MANY PSYCHICS, at some point, begin to recognize the belief of reincarnation. If it wasn't a part of their belief systems to start, there is often a turning point where the idea becomes more solidified as part of their core thinking. For many of us, our Christian background seemingly doesn't support the thought of reincarnation or the idea of past lives. The idea of one life and one death is indoctrinated into us from a very young age. However, there is a contradiction. Jesus Christ himself "rises again"; ultimately, he reincarnates and his disciple, Mary, tells us of the occasion. This is neither the first nor last contradiction in the Bible, but it does illustrate a point. Even those who have been instructed to believe that reincarnation doesn't exist, actually buy into it to a certain point. But, back to the issue at hand. You very well may, over time and over several readings, come across what you know to be a past life vision/scene. You'll know it when it happens, and it will happen. At that point, you may have to address one of two different theories.

▶ Theory 1: Even though we may be *perceiving* a past life, we may just be tapping into the universal consciousness and pulling information relevant to the person, but not, individually theirs. This may be to show us a karmic aspect that is relevant in this lifetime to the person you are reading for. For instance, you may have a vision of a slave owner beating his or her slaves in an act of domination. If, working with this theory, this comes up; you may need to convey the idea of the individual being far too hard on those around him. He may need to be more encouraging and supportive and understanding to have far more productive relationships.

▶ Theory 2: The past life scene being perceived is a literal vision and not one to be interpreted. If you were to see, say, a person tending sheep, you would announce that the person being read for was a shepherd. In this concept, the actual events being portrayed are concluded to be the actual events of the past life. I try to stay away from interpretation as much as I can, only sticking to the information given to me, so I tend to work with this theory. However, you will not only have to search your soul and feel what is right, but also see how your psychic gifts develop. Maybe both theories are right, but certain psychics work with metaphor and analogy and others literal scenes.

More than personal experience, I came to believe in past lives from research and my work in hypnotic past life regression. Upon study, I found that children all over the world, regardless of cultural background, religion, or economic class, reported memories of past lives with other families, often in vastly different geographic locations. The information that was reported was noted from very young children who would not, otherwise, have had knowledge of landmarks, names, or language. Further, a few years ago I became a board-certified hypnotherapist. Due to my interest in past lives, I took additional interest and training in past-life regressions that are performed in hypnosis. Through these sessions, I have heard various clients speak of lands that they have never visited and been given details regarding history that neither I, nor they, had current knowledge of. Only after research did we find out the information to be true. Because of these instances, I've become a firm believer in past lives and reincarnation.

©istockphoto.com/Markus Seidel

Whether or not you make past lives a part of your belief, you do need to acknowledge that they are a major part of several world cultures. It's pretty well known that Buddhists and Hindus believe in the idea of reincarnation equally. They believe that a soul evolves due to its karmic influence from life to life. Ultimately, the ideal is for the soul to become enlightened. In this ideology, the soul could and can move forward and backward in different forms. For example, in one life a soul may be an insect. Then, moving forward in evolution, a dog, and then later, in another life, human. Of course the human could then provide a karmic choice and de-evolve in the next life to a goat. Ancient Greek philosophers also taught the idea of past lives. Plato and Socrates both taught the concepts of reincarnation.

As I mentioned above, in the discussion of the Buddhist idea of reincarnation, karma often plays an important role in the concept of many lives. Karma is the concept that all things that we do and say have a cause and effect. The idea originated in ancient India, but the concept has been integrated throughout various religions and philosophies. For example, Christianity includes the idea of "you reap what you sow." Ultimately, karma is neither good nor bad. It's a simple product of your own free will. And because you, and only you, make your own choices, the result is the influence or the "karmic" destiny. However, the destiny may be immediate or it may be quite delayed, as in affecting another lifetime.

If you choose to integrate the idea and belief of past lives into your readings, you will more than likely have to address someone who believes to have had an extraordinary past life. Unfortunately, people connect to major points and major players in history. Typically, this is due to our cultural fascination with celebrity. And because of this, they feel an affinity for that time period or a well-known individual within that timeframe. I'll call it the "King Tut" syndrome. It's a lovely fantasy to believe that we were someone spectacular in history. Or perhaps to, at least, believe that we witnessed a major turning point in our human evolution. The simple fact of the matter is that this just isn't the case. The world, as we know it, was built by laborers, farmers, peasants, slaves, and the like. And, the majority of us did that kind of work to perpetuate the species and develop countries. So, in most cases, we were

not Cleopatra, King Arthur, or the Emperor of Japan. Because those people are highly focused on in the media and in our history we feel a connection, but often that connection is simply more geographic than anything else.

Another way to address past lives is to have a hypnotic past-life regression. There has been an insurgence of psychics choosing to study hypnosis to provide these regressions so clients may see, for themselves, their own past lives. I have gone through that training and find that it is a wonderful complement to the information that I get in readings. If you choose to add this to your journey, make sure you find someone who really has a background in the hypnosis industry. Work to not only provide past-life readings but to also address other issues (weight and phobias for example) hypnotically as well.

©istockphoto.com/Amanda Lewis

The "Other Side"

THERE IS A LOT OF SPECULATION about the "other side" or "home" (as I prefer to call it). As you develop your psychic abilities, you'll have more opportunity to become familiar with the other side and its workings. More often than not, the other side is perceived as a different dimension, not a place that resides up in the sky amidst the clouds. It is a place where energy and souls are very much connected to us (they move and shift with us); however, they are out of our physical site due to vibration differences. Because of this vibrational difference, they have to slow themselves down a great deal to communicate and connect with us.

A point that you will quickly come to understand is that the other side is *infinite.* What I mean by this is that those who we may be quite close to on this side don't necessarily stick with us so closely on the other side. We don't have to be with our spouse every moment of time because time, again, is *infinite.* I don't think it's a concept that our human brains can fully comprehend. I often get asked the question: "Are my mom and dad together on the other side?" It's a wonderful, heartfelt question, but the answer is often different than expected. It's not that we don't have or want the same relationships with those we are here with on Earth, but we need to also reconnect with other souls on the other side. The commitment of marriage is not necessary on the other side. Again, because all things are forever and perpetual, marriage is not necessary or warranted. Even our marriage vows reflect that idea to some extent saying, "until death do us part." After all, we continue to evolve and grow at home, so it would only be to our benefit to experience all people and personalities on the other side.

With the understanding that the other side vibrates at a higher level, we have to also understand that timing is perceived differently there. There are two different ways that this can impact readings. The first being their communications in reference to timeframes of happenings for future events. The second is after a soul crosses over. Regarding the impact on readings, be aware that our days are moments to them. Likewise, years are only weeks. Because of this, when searching for insight and information regarding the timing for events, be *very* sure if you get a month or date that it is in the *year* that you perceive. You may want to ask your guides or those you are connecting to, psychically, for more information around the timing. I know that, even after 20 years of providing readings, I still sometimes miss on the timing of events. Of course, part of that ties back to our free will, but I take the ownership on it as well. As I mentioned, this can also impact mediumistic communication. After we cross over, we go through a period of review and acclimation to the other side. Until we are comfortable and accepting of the life we just led, here on Earth, we remain there being nurtured by other souls. Because the soul has free will, we can stay in that process until we are ready to move on and further experience the other side. The soul may choose to remain there for only a bit or may opt to linger there for a few of our years. It's really what is right for the individual and what they feel comfortable with. Because of this, it may be difficult to reach someone who has recently passed over. As they vibrate differently, they may feel they have been in review for only moments, but to us it is a year. It's something to remember when trying to connect with a loved one on the other side.

Remember, too, that those on the other side still have their own personalities, senses of humor, likes and dislikes. We are not assimilated into a neutral, unfeeling, comprehensive being. We still incorporate our opinions; however, we have a broader viewpoint and perspective on many things. Because of that, some opinions will change once we go home, but we still are individuals. So many people share with me the last moments with a loved one not being ideal. Sometimes there was a fight. Or a family member wasn't able to get back home in time for the passing. No matter what the circumstance, know that the souls on the other side love you and are completely capable of forgiveness as well! Although, they rarely need to forgive as they have that broader understanding for why things happened the way they did. If we didn't hold on to these character traits, we'd lose our humanity and ultimately ourselves.

Although those who have crossed over have all things provided for, as we are released from the physical body there is still the desire to *do* something. After we recuperate from our transition, there are projects and jobs to do. The jobs are as various as the individuals on the other side. If you have a desire to write, there are record keepers maintaining copious notes regarding what transpires on Earth. If you are a history buff, you can work in the various historical libraries. If you loved carpentry during your physical life, you can build whatever you desire back at home. Although we can create anything we need or want with our minds on the other side, there is never a question about the joy of creating with raw materials. Of course, some souls choose to become spirit guides and work to assist us back here on Earth. Needless to say, that takes a great deal of training and dedication!

Psychic Places

THERE ARE MANY REPORTED psychic "places" all around the world. Here in the United States there are several. But beyond those more regional to us, we find that many people have a connection to various places globally. For instance, we often hear of people having a spiritual or psychic experience on a trip to India. Or an individual may find a deeper connection when visiting the Vatican in Italy. I believe that there is something to these psychic places. Additionally, I think that there is something there to explore and study. Perhaps it's the formations of rock and stone. Perhaps it is what has transpired there in history imprinting the land. Whatever the case, those on their psychic journey tend to find a vibrational connection to these places.

There is a theory that one of the components of a psychic place is the stone granite. Because granite is mainly composed of quartz, its energies innately amplify all other energies around it. So, any psychic abilities are boosted by its presence. However, granite also has other minerals that assist its psychic enhancement energies. Additionally, it helps balance one's personality and keep them open to experiences. Further, granite in its composition is a very strong and durable rock. All of these things in combination make granite not only a practical and useful construction tool, but also a draw for divine communications.

Another theory in the paranormal realm is the "Stone Tape Theory". This theory proposes that after a tragic, dramatic, or emotional event that the energy from the event is imprinted on the stones in the geographic location of the scene. Then, over the course of time, the event replays, like a tape or movie, projecting itself, over and over under certain circumstances. Therefore what we perceive as "ghosts" appear or are heard. Unfortunately, there isn't any scientific evidence that this theory is correct; however, reports of "residual hauntings" occur time and time again. This may be the reason.

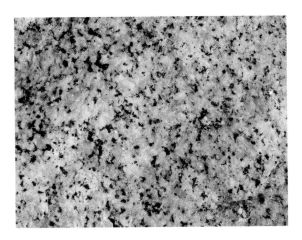

Another theory around psychic places is the existence of an "energy vortex." An energy vortex is a geographic area where there is an intense condensation of psychic/spiritual/dimensional energy. Often psychically perceived as a whirling, tornado-shaped mass, this vortex allows for deep, soulful connections and communications to be made. Not only do you feel deeply connected to the higher consciousness, but also there is the rejuvenation factor that goes along with the vortex. Some believe that the energy vortex is created due to underground magnetism or electrical charges. Unfortunately, there is no scientific evidence to conclude this to be true. However, like many things around metaphysics, that doesn't necessarily disprove anything. Some people in well-known vortexes feel light headed, tingly, may hallucinate and/or have a pronounced feeling of well-being. Others claim to not physically feel anything, but simply regain calm that has eluded them in the day-to-day life.

Alfred Watkins

Yet another thing we should consider when researching psychic places is the existence of *ley lines*. Here again, ley lines are not scientifically proven. They are only given a theorized existence. The metaphysical idea around ley lines is that they are unseen, energetic lines between distinct locations. At the intersections of these lines lie great psychic energies. The idea of ley lines is relatively new. A man by the name of Alfred Watkins of England noticed paths between hilltops one afternoon when out riding a horse. From there, it is told that he had a "vision" of these energetic lines criss-crossing the entire Earth. In the books *Early British Trackways* and *The Old Straight Track,* Mr. Watkins published his ideas about ley lines and his experiences. Unfortunately, the books were met with a negative response.

One well-known, distinguishable psychic place is Stonehenge in Wiltshire, UK. Some believe that Stonehenge was built by our ancestors as a ritual burial ground. Others believe it to be a sacred Druidic ritual site. Most commonly it is believed to be a calendar. Either way, people who have visited the site have been said to experience psychic energies. Some believe that Stonehenge is at an intersection of ley lines, and, because of this, a vortex exists. Others believe that because the ancient elders (Druidic or otherwise) have conducted such important ceremonies there, that the ground itself is charged with magical and mystical energies opening psychic abilities and healing physical maladies.

Others still believe that Stonehenge may have been used as a great astrological observatory, and because of that the stones themselves are charged with future-telling properties. Here again, we run into theory and science having little, if any, correlating explanation. Either way, we can all agree that Stonehenge is one of the great mysteries of the world.

Now, in my estimation, the greatest of all psychic places would be the astral plane. The astral plane does not exist in the physical world, but rather in the etheric dimensions. In theory, this is where the souls on the other side reside and can communicate with the physical world. Of course, during astral travel/projection (discussed in Chapter 5) the individual on the Earth plane can access the astral plane. Interestingly enough, in some experiments of the astral plane, individuals neutrally examined could consciously connect with others (people) in the physical world. They were able to identify the clothing worn and what conversations took place in the target area.

Sedona, Arizona is another believed psychic location where people claim multiple energy vortexes (seven are readily known and can be toured formally or by oneself) exist. The ideas of ley lines also create the energies to support and expand psychic abilities. Because of the reported energy grid within the Sedona area, there are various New Age centers and a high volume of psychics that work in the region. In addition, Sedona was one location of the Harmonic Convergence, which occurred in 1987. This event was the brainchild of author Jose Arguelles and was held on August 16th and 17th, with the dates based on the alignment of the planets as stated by the Mayan calendar. Other locations noted as psychic sites are Mount Shasta, Stonehenge, and Bloomington, Indiana, among others.

Psychics and Religion

I OFTEN GET ASKED ABOUT my religious affiliation. That question is quickly followed by how I reconcile my Christian background with what I have chosen to do for a living. Fortunately for me, I was born with a pretty thick skin and recognize that the question is more about curiosity rather than judgment. As you work on and develop your psychic abilities, be ready for this question *if* you choose to come out of the psychic closet. More often than not, people are curious, but it may come out slightly hostile.

When you speak with others following the same path or those who are professional psychics, you're going to find a deep, deep faith in what they do and often that transfers over into their personal faith base. Although, you may find that many psychics would consider themselves "spiritual" rather than religious. So, it may seem a little ambiguous at first, but when you dig deeper, you're going to find that they have often melded various religious beliefs and pulled together their own, personal belief system. Because of this, many psychics are quite versed on various theology and philosophy. At a minimum, it's due to wanting to respect the clients and public that they may encounter. But, for most, it's due to their personal spiritual journey.

A wonderful example of a psychic who had an incredibly deep faith was Edgar Cayce. Although I spoke about him in the first chapter, Mr. Cayce deserves a lot of respect and study. It's well known and highly documented that Mr. Cayce had a deep, penetrating faith in Christianity. He was a devout member of the Disciples of Christ (a protestant denomination) throughout his entire life, read the Bible each year, and taught at Sunday school. No argument could be made against Mr. Cayce's dedication to his religion. In addition, he recruited missionaries to assist in the building of churches. However, due to his strong conviction in the Christian faith, he struggled a great deal reconciling his psychic abilities with how they integrated with his religious upbringing. This is something that many, many psychics wrestle with.

I consider myself to be an "enhanced Christian." The meaning of that has many, many layers. First and foremost, I want to honor and respect my Christian background. I was baptized Christian (Lutheran more specifically) and certainly grew up indoctrinated into that idea. However, through my studies, I learned about different ideas, faiths, and philosophies. In addition, I discovered how different *cultures* explored their faith and religion. This also deepened my faith. Because of this, I felt that I still, fundamentally, based my faith on my Christian background; however, I incorporated several different aspects of other religions into my belief system. For instance, I adore rosaries and believe in the power within them. However, I also assimilated the idea of reincarnation and meditation into my day-to-day faith. Because of the integration, I embrace my Christian heritage but don't limit myself to it.

Now, when we look at the idea of psychics and what the Bible says about them, we run into a lot of conflicting material. Many of us are familiar with the verse in the Bible that mentions "testing" or "trying" a psychic (or spirit/ghost or medium depending on the translation) to see if he is valid and of "God" (I put God in quotes not to question validity, but to honestly quote the passage). However, the *entire* Bible is based on having "faith" in God and trusting that He (and I use the male pronoun as it is used in the Bible) is watching over you and communicating with you in only ways that can be understood by the divine. Testing God does not bode well for any mortal man or woman. However, putting the idea of testing God aside, what are we to say if a psychic is accurate and proven to be true? Does that mean that he is doing God's will and communicating something from the divine? Would that be righteous and in line with the testament of the Bible? Just something to consider.

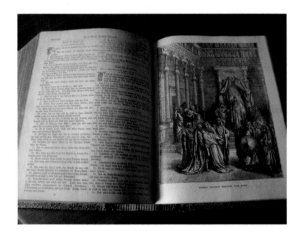

Further, you'll find that many of the major players in the Bible prophesied and were given messages from angels. You can read these stories time and time again in various chapters. Jesus himself, gave the prophesy of his own death. So, again we find a conflict of information. Doesn't it say in John 14:12: "I tell you the truth, anyone who has faith in me (Jesus) will do what I have been doing. He will do even greater things than these, because I am going to the Father." So, if Christ himself was predicting the future and said that we *will* do these things (ultimately encouraging us), why do some followers of the Christian doctrine condemn us and call us sinful? The simple answer is this: Some messages are interpreted as literal and others as analogy or metaphor. The sad thing is that no one can agree what is what. And, unfortunately, you'll find that how things are interpreted often coincide with what is convenient and just in *one* individual's eyes.

Yet another thing to consider is determining the difference between a prophet and a psychic. Is it semantics only? In my estimation, the words have the same meaning. But that is my opinion. However, the idea of a prophet is embraced by the Christian doctrine where the word *psychic*, for many fundamentalist Christians, aligns itself with the Devil. As I mentioned above, Jesus Christ predicted future events and counseled the community. Essentially, isn't that what a psychic does? They work to assist those around them to find their path and connect their soul with the divine. One may argue that a prophet works to connect God to a community where a psychic works one on one, individually. Allow yourself, when pondering your development to consider all these various things. How does your faith integrate with your psychic abilities?

Psychics in Paranormal Investigations

SOMETIMES PSYCHICS CHOOSE to become involved in paranormal investigations. Although many psychics don't care to delve into the paranormal and remain more in the spiritual or metaphsical, currently, it's a popular pursuit and is worth consideration. However, I don't recommend that beginning psychics delve into this exploration. After much study, research, and thought, only then should you consider your options and determine if this is part of your path. If you choose to work in the paranormal realms, bear in mind that you may come across some energies and psychic impressions that are troublesome. Although it isn't always the case, often paranormal activity and mental health issues go hand in hand. And, as a psychic in an investigation, you may open yourself up to that and that can be painful. However, there are many upsides to utilizing your psychic abilities on an investigation. During an investigation, keeping yourself aptly protected, you can be a radar for activity, spirit presence, and psychic information. All of which can assist the science of paranormal investigation bringing us all closer to more answers. If you are interested in ghost hunting, I highly recommend *Picture Yourself Ghost Hunting.*

Psychic Vampires

A "HOT TOPIC" RIGHT NOW is speaking to psychic vampires. *Psychic vampires* are those who consciously, or, most often, subconsciously, seem to pull energy from another. We all know of a friend or family member that, after spending time with them, we feel exhausted. Whether we were simply having coffee or exercising at the gym, we need to physically retire and recuperate after seeing them. This, more than likely, is the subconscious psychic vampire. However, there are psychic vampires out there who are very much aware of their need to draw energy from other living creatures. Some do this with permission. They will actually ask to "feed" off another to gain strength and energy in their own bodies/lives. Sometimes, this assists in a healing process. My friend, writer and author Michelle Belanger (*Sacred Hunger, Psychic Energy Codex,* and many more), has written about her experiences with psychic vampirism. Overall, I suggest using the methods mentioned in the psychic protection chapter to block out any subconscious psychic vampire from extinguishing your energy, psychic or otherwise.

Psychic Kids

GROWING UP AS A PSYCHIC kid really wasn't all that different from any other childhood experience. Of course, I didn't know any different. And neither will your child if you determine that your son or daughter is having psychic experiences. Remember that the most important thing is to keep your child *a child.* Although the experiences range from exciting to scary to enlightening, for both the parent and child, it's important to not push anyone into anything, no matter what the predisposition is. Another thing, as a parent, remember it's important to never seem thrown off or frightened regarding what your child is going through. Even if you may be a bit hesitant or fearful, find a professional and consult with them.

The best suggestion that I can give any parent of a psychic child is to educate and inform herself of all things psychic. Learn what your child may be experiencing. Find out how things come through and present themselves to psychics. Open up to techniques that can be taught to your child if your child approaches you for advice. Additionally, be hyper aware of anything that has a supernatural, paranormal, or psychic spin on it. Too often children become mislead by what Hollywood and the media portray around psychic abilities. Unfortunately, this can bring on an incorrect expectation of what those with psychic skills experience.

As I mentioned in an earlier chapter, a "hot" term in the arena of psychic kids is the idea of "indigo kids/children". The expression "indigo kids" describes children that seem to have a high predisposition of psychic ability from a very young age. They seem to have a deep love of earth, are deeply sensitive and have a great deal of frustration with those individuals who are not able or choose not to express their deepest, soulful feelings. The term "indigo child" comes from those psychically able to view the auras around people. It was found that around these children there was a deep, indigo blue aura. Although the term originated in the 1970s, it wasn't until the 1990s that the term and idea gained popularity.

Children are amazing and wonderful, and part of that brilliance is their imagination. What is often difficult for a parent to discern is if the child is really, truly having a psychic experience or if it is imaginary. Really, when it comes down to it, you can readily conclude what is truly happening and what may only be in the mind of the child.

First and foremost, if a child comes to you mentioning information that is directly related to you or the family that she would have no way of knowing (something that wouldn't be overheard or seen in video or picture), you may want to take that seriously. If the child mentions a name that is quite unusual and isn't part of a cartoon, story, or internet character, you may want to delve further. However, if the youngster mentions a name then tells you a story that is even *remotely* similar to something that he may have come across, let it go. Don't go looking for your child to be psychic. And certainly don't lead the child, providing him information to "tune in" to. Honestly, I wouldn't encourage children in the slightest *unless* they come to you, unsolicited, without influence of you (and remember, seeing a demonstration, real or fiction and giving it any sort of praise may have quite an influence as children want the approval of their parents), TV, movies, or friends.

Many parents ask me about their child's "invisible friend," and if it might be a spirit guide/loved one on the other side. The simple answer is yes, it certainly *could* be. However, use good judgment and prudence. Just like any other psychic experience, ask questions. Find out if it has similarities to any cartoon or movie, recent or otherwise.

Ask if this "friend" is kind or mean. Ask about the age of the "friend." If there is a correlation, don't worry about it or try to discourage your child. Remember, the psychology around a kid having an invisible friend is completely healthy and fine. However, if you don't seem to find any evidence of media or storytelling, then *do* look into the possibility of your child connecting with the other side. He or she may be connecting with a passed family member. This is easily verifiable and validated. However, if information starts coming through that is more predictive in nature, the child may very well be speaking with a spirit guide, either hers or yours. The bottom line, like with anything else, is to use good, common sense.

We have to remember that children, simply by their age, have a heightened psychic connection and therefore have more psychic experiences. Because they are so young and haven't had the societal constrictions placed upon them (yet), they have brilliantly open minds and the other side finds many, many ways to communicate with them. Further, because they are closer to the other side, from a timeline stance (they haven't been on Earth as long), children have a closer connection with the other side, remembering how they connect and communicate, even if only on a subconscious level. They haven't had all the other "trappings" of life fill their little minds and muddy up their psychic side.

Remember, if you feel that your child, or a child you know, may be having psychic experiences, he may not have the words to inform you. Without having the life experience, sometimes it's a struggle for the child to explain what happened. In cases such as these, I bring out crayons, colored pencils, and a drawing pad. Quite frequently, a child can show you, with amazing detail, the visual aspect of what happened. Then, from the portrayal, you can then ask more specific questions and really drill down on what transpired. Not only are you engaging the child to show what happened, but you may also get the feelings of the child when the episode happened. You may find that he portrays himself with a smile on his face. Or, it may be fear.

Keep in mind, if your child is scared or frightened by a psychic event, reinforce safety. Use the psychic protection techniques found in Chapter 7. Explain to your child how she *will* be protected and that her fears can be put aside. Your tone, conviction, and belief may be more comforting than anything. Another wonderful tool that children seem to really respond well to is the use of a Native American dream catcher. Although these tools are meant to inhibit bad dreams, kids are familiar with them and seem to find great solace using them for psychic protection as well.

©istockphoto.com/DawnPoland

Conclusion

MORE THAN ANYTHING, I want to thank you for investing in yourself and investing in this book. I know this is a long-term commitment, that sometimes, may not be entirely comfortable. As with anything of a spiritual nature, we have to reconcile things within ourselves that may not be easy or fun. And, often, we need to dig deep to find answers, going into our past while still looking ahead to gain ground. This is a tough row to hoe, but you can do this! There is a lot of information out there and this is just a start. Don't overwhelm yourself. YOU, TOO, ARE PSYCHIC!

Remember that no one is perfect. And there isn't one simple answer to any spiritual or psychic topic. Take what you learn and evaluate it. Decide if it works for you. Even if it works for you for a day, it's worthwhile. If you find it contrary, it's okay! Retain it as information and you'll learn where it fits some other time. If an exercise doesn't work for you the first time, try it again next week. Or next month. As you grow and expand upon your psychic abilities, you're going to find that you're constantly changing and expanding not only your psychic self but also your personal philosophy.

There are many people who may be skeptical about what you learn and what you do psychically. However, there are just as many that will embrace and encourage your efforts. Focus on the good, supporting crowd. There's plenty of time for you to deal with those who may question your abilities and intensions. This venture is about you and what you want to accomplish. Don't let ego or others get in the way of those accomplishments. On this journey, you'll learn more about yourself than you ever dreamed imaginable!

I've said it before, but it bears repeating, EVERYONE is psychic. You can do all those things that the psychics on TV can do, and, more than likely, you'll do far better! This book gives you points to leap off of. Take it and dive in! Remember that psychic abilities are not about testing and trials. They are about faith and belief. Believe in yourself. Believe and trust in the information you receive. I have frequently said that I don't know anything about anything in my life with the exception of that information that comes in a reading. That's the stuff I'm sure about.

If anything feels awkward or wrong in your studies, don't go there. It's not for you. That doesn't mean that you forget it, you just put it away and return to it when the timing is right. Pushing yourself through a frightening experience will not gain you any ground. We, as psychics, have to proceed with caution. As we use our bodies as an antenna, we have to heed our personal security system. But, remember that frustration and fear are two distinct emotions. Frustration reminds us to do something differently that what we are doing currently. Fear means to move away or stop.

Don't let yourself burn out. It's so exciting to gain ground psychically and want to only pursue more and more. But, folks, I'm here to tell you, that leads to imbalance. And when a psychic is out of balance, the psychic information will stop. Or, at best, it will trickle in. If that happens, you're no good to anyone, including yourself.

Take baby steps. Before long those baby steps will turn into strides. Remember that although you are working energetically, it's your body that houses that energy and has to keep up with the exploration. So, too much too soon leads to burn out. It's like taking a remote control that requires AA batteries and hooking it up to a car battery. It just isn't going to have the capacity. Take your time. Enjoy the ride.

I look forward to hearing from you as to your new tips and techniques that YOU have discovered for yourself! Any teacher, in any subject, hopes for her students to become more than what she has become. Share your journey! It's part of the growth process. Maybe, next it will be your story that we all hear about!

painting by Cindy Kadelski

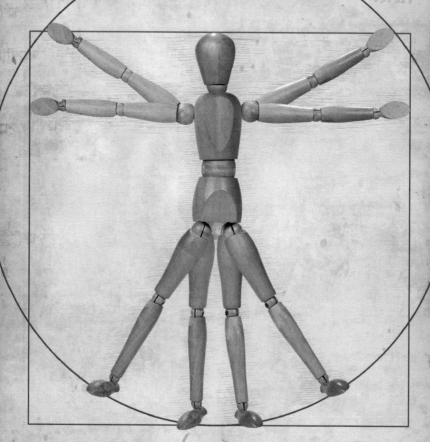

Resources

THE FOLLOWING IS A LIST of resources to help you further your psychic development.

Locations/Websites

The Learning Annex

www.learningannex.com

The Learning Annex not only has online psychic development classes, but also, frequently, has physical, in-person classes you can register for in your area. Costs vary.

The Center

www.echobodine.com

Echo Bodine is a wonderful psychic and a dear friend of mine. She created The Center (MN) to hold not only classes on psychic development, but also healing touch. She is a well-known psychic and author and I recommend her constantly.

Association for Research and Enlightenment

www.edgarcayce.org

Edgar Cayce, one of the world's best-known psychics, founded this not-for-profit organization in 1931. To this day it continues to be one of the foremost facilities to educate and inform the public on psychism. Classes and events are ongoing and there are local branches nationwide.

Lily Dale Assembly

www.lilydaleassembly.com

The Lily Dale Assembly (FL) is a center for spiritual development. All of the members subscribe to the Spiritualist church. They are known to have some of the most accurate and well-known psychics in their midst. Workshops, lectures, and readings are all provided in this gated community.

Association of Unity Churches

www.unity.org

Unity churches are nationwide and well known for embracing the spirituality of all people. Although Christian based, they have their hearts and minds open to all things spiritual. Noted for having speakers such as Gregg Braden, James Twyman, and Michael Beckwith.

Beliefnet.com

www.beliefnet.com

Beliefnet's mission is to provide an online resource for ALL things spiritual. Topics such as angels, holistic living, and meditation are predominant on this website. Not only are there marvelous articles, but also video and audio clips!

Meetup.com

www.meetup.com

Although a website for all interests, Meetup.com has many psychic development groups, both online and in person all over the country. Simply by entering your interest and location, the website will find groups close to you that match your interest level. Great for group support!

Books

Ancient Teachings for Beginners

Doug DeLong

I love this book, as I'm a big fan of practical application. And this book doles it out. I very much appreciate Mr. DeLong's effort in writing useful techniques that anyone can utilize.

The Gift

Echo Bodine

I remember when this book came out and how *proud* I was of Echo for writing it. Echo let everyone know what psychism is, and, most importantly, what it is not. It's a wonderful book with personal stories and great information.

The Encyclopedic Psychic Dictionary

June Bletzer, Ph.D.

This isn't a story or technique book, per say. This book is thousands of entries on all things psychic and metaphysical. If you want a great reference book, this is it.

Small Mediums at Large

Terri Iacuzzo

One of my all-time favorite books, Terri writes about her real-life trials and tribulations growing up psychic in a very psychic family. If you want to understand that you are not alone on this journey, search out this book and gain some wonderful insight!

Tarot Plain and Simple

Anthony Louis

If you are drawn to study Tarot, this book is for you. I think I've purchased this book over a dozen times and handed it out to those starting on their personal path with Tarot. A great beginning book.

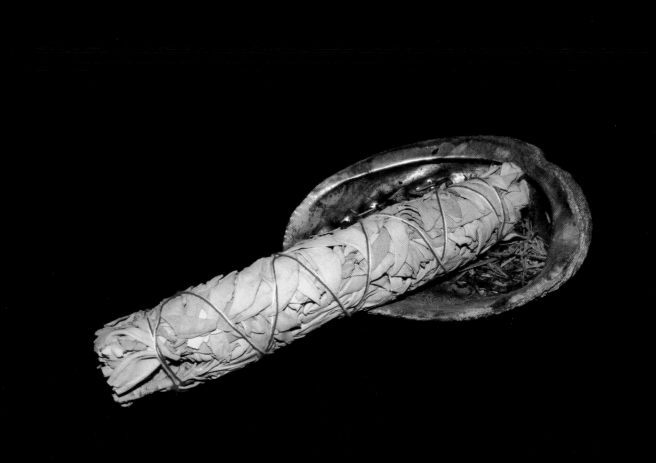

The DVD

IN ADDITION TO THE BOOK, I have included a DVD to delve a bit deeper into various topics. You'll get a feel of how I do things and work some of the "tools" in the psychic trade.

Clearing Space

The first segment is dedicated to clearing space and protection exercises. You'll notice that I use a few different physical tools to help with the process. Sage, a feather, and salt are frequently used tools (shown in the video) in clearing space. In the video, I walk you through the process of lighting the sage and then wafting the sage smoke around the area. You can also use the smoke of the sage to cleanse the energetic body to clear negative energies that may have attached to you.

I also speak to using salt for protection from negativity. In the same way sage and smudging clears space, salt dissipates negative emotions and energies. It's another tool to use to protect the physical body and the areas around you. The benefit of salt is that it can be purchased at any number of locations and easily carried on the body at any time.

Tarot

In the second segment of the DVD, I work with you on Tarot readings. Not only do I show you a simple Tarot spread, but speak to you on how to store your cards, shuffling, terminology, and reversed card positions. Remember, as you work with the cards, you'll find what you prefer in your own personal readings. Tarot, frequently, is a wonderful "leap off" point for the tuning in to your own psychic abilities.

Within the reading, I work with you to explain how the interpretation of the card and the placement of the cards within the spread work together, simultaneously, to give you the reading. Walking you through each position in a "Celtic Cross" spread I explain to you what each placement means in the reading as I pull cards for myself. During this section, you'll learn how to walk through a reading and ultimately put the different pieces of the Tarot together!

Sample Reading

Providing a sample reading for you to see and understand, you'll gain some insight, in this segment of the DVD, into how you may want to provide readings for others. This section is about you gaining confidence in what you receive as a psychic, and being confident to speak to the information that comes through from Spirit. Liz, the recipient of the reading, has never had a reading before, so not only do you see how I choose to provide a reading, but you can get a first hand account of her hesitations, questions, and reactions.

You'll hear me guiding Liz on how to formulate questions for those of you who would like to *receive* a reading as well. Additionally, this guidance helps you assist your potential clients to get the most from a reading. I stress not being led by the person asking for insight and I work with you to get specific questions without being swayed by personal information that may come out in a reading.

Frequently Asked Questions

Lastly, I address several questions that I've been asked personally, publicly, and privately. Not only do I give you answers to basic psychic ability questions, but also talk to you about why I took on this project, and other information on how I came to this path. You'll come to understand, through the questions presented, that although I have been pursuing the psychic world for 20+ years, I admittedly still have many questions myself.

This segment explains to you more of how I receive information, what I perceive the other side to be like, and various personal opinions. Not all of this information may be identical to your thoughts and feelings on any given subject, but, it will give you food for thought and get you thinking about where you are on these topics.

©istockphoto.com/Rob Blackburn

©istockphoto.com/sandramo

Glossary

angel

A divinely created creature that exists for the glorification of God. Angels never live a human life but may take human form to intercede on the divine's behalf.

animal totem

The energy/spirit of a particular animal that works, on another plane, on an individual's (human) behalf.

astral projection

Projection of the soul out of the physical body into the astral plane.

aura

The energetic emanation of the physical body that is fed by the chakras.

automatic writing

A psychic ability where an individual channels information, unknown to them, through a writing device (pencil, pen, computer, etc.).

bilocation
The projection of the soul, out of the physical body, to another physical place.

chakra
An energy wheel that feeds the aura and maintains the energetic body keeping it in balance.

channeling
When a psychic utilizes an ability to gain information that is not otherwise known by the psychic his/herself through one of the 4 physical human senses.

clairaudience
One of the four psychic abilities—in this case, where the psychic gains information through psychic hearing.

clairgustance
One of the four psychic abilities where the psychic gains information through psychic taste and/or smell.

clairsentience
One of the four psychic abilities where the psychic gains information through psychic feeling/empathy.

clairvoyance
One of the four psychic abilities where the psychic gains information through psychic sight.

cold reading
A technique used by fraudulent psychics where they gain information through various techniques that are not psychic in nature. Examples would be observing body language, noticing a dialect, etc.

divine connection
The connection between humans and their personal version of the divine whether it be a God, Goddess, nature, etc.

discernment
A term used by the Bible and seen as a gift from God (Christian), where a human being has the ability to determine good spirits from bad spirits.

doppelganger
The spirit form or ghost of a living, corporeal human being. Lately, this term has been used less formally to simply mean a look alike of another person.

dowsing
Using a tool (often a pendulum or divining rods) to find answers to a question. The term dowsing, in the past, has been limited to the ability of finding water, but the term has broadened over time.

energy vortex
A large, unseen, condensed, whirling, tornado-like psychic energy that is often connected with a geographic location.

enlightenment
The epitome of divine connection and the balance between the physical and etheric bodies.

etheric body
The human energy field that is connected to the physical body. Often portrayed as a halo around the body.

free will
A God-given right that all human beings can make choices and decisions for themselves that may potentially be sinful or against their best interest.

ghost
A discarnate, Earth-bound spirit.

hot reading
Providing a faux "psychic" reading using prior knowledge.

I Ching
The Chinese "Book of Changes" that hopes to foretell coming events.

imagination
The aspect of the mind that creates out of education, experience, and expansion.

intuition
The voice within, guided by the divine, which gives us inner knowledge. Sometimes thought of as the "gut" feeling.

leading
Giving a psychic too much information so they are "led" in a direction and lose their objectivity.

ley lines
Nonphysical lines that possibly exist connecting energy strongholds on Earth.

meditation
Going into a deep state of relaxation where the mind opens up and opens awareness.

mediumship
Connecting to human spirits, on the other side, and communicating messages.

metaphysics
The study of being and knowing and the transcendence therein.

New Age
A term that can pertain to a spiritual movement combined with a study of metaphysics.

numerology
The study of numbers and the patterns within them that affect the physical world.

other side
A term that is often used for "heaven" or where spirits go after passing from the physical world.

palmistry
Divination using the lines on the hand.

paranormal
Things that are beyond the "normal" five senses.

past life/lives
The idea that the soul lives many lives and that we not only have the current life we are living, but also prior lives.

pendulum
A dowsing tool that is some form of string or chain with a heavier object at the end.

prophesy
Prediction of the future typically through a vision given to an individual.

psychic
Someone who is able, through one of the four psychic abilities, to gain information beyond using one (or more) of the five senses.

psychic accuracy
The statistic of accuracy that a psychic has through his or her predictions.

psychic protection
Protection for oneself from psychic energies.

psychic reading
A session given by a psychic for another.

psychic validation
The confirmation of a prediction that a psychic has made.

psychic vampire
An individual who draws energy from one person into himself, sometimes exhausting the source.

psychism
The study and practice of being psychic.

psychometry
The psychic procedure of gaining psychic information by touching and/or feeling an object.

querent
The person requesting a psychic reading.

reincarnation
The idea that we do not live only one life here on Earth. It's the concept that we live many lives.

remote viewing
Projection of the soul, out of the body, to another physical place.

seer
Another word for psychic or prophet.

shaman
An individual who works as a healer and spiritual leader typically in indigenous tribes.

silver cord
The connection that is not perceived in the physical, but often seen by psychics, that connects humans to the divine and to each other.

Spirit
The term that is used as a synonym for the soul or used as the term for a soul that has passed over but still visits and communicates with those here on Earth.

spirit guide
A soul, on the other side, that assists humans, here on Earth, on their personal and soulful paths.

spirituality
The concept and focus of working on the spirit/soul.

soul
The consciousness, that is immortal and housed by the physical, of every living being.

Tarot
A divination tool that typically consists of 78 cards divided up into the Major Arcana and Minor Arcana.

Tarot spread
How Tarot cards are laid out to give insight on past, present, and future events.

telepathy
Reading another individual's mind.

trance mediumship
Mediumship that is obtained through a deep, sleeplike state. It's often said that the individual performing such a session is unaware of what is being conveyed.

vision
The psychic communication that comes through clairvoyance.

visualization
Creating an image within the mind.

Index

License Agreement/Notice of Limited Warranty

By opening the sealed disc container in this book, you agree to the following terms and conditions. If, upon reading the following license agreement and notice of limited warranty, you cannot agree to the terms and conditions set forth, return the unused book with unopened disc to the place where you purchased it for a refund.

License:

The enclosed software is copyrighted by the copyright holder(s) indicated on the software disc. You are licensed to copy the software onto a single computer for use by a single user and to a backup disc. You may not reproduce, make copies, or distribute copies or rent or lease the software in whole or in part, except with written permission of the copyright holder(s). You may transfer the enclosed disc only together with this license, and only if you destroy all other copies of the software and the transferee agrees to the terms of the license. You may not decompile, reverse assemble, or reverse engineer the software.

Notice of Limited Warranty:

The enclosed disc is warranted by Course Technology to be free of physical defects in materials and workmanship for a period of sixty (60) days from end user's purchase of the book/disc combination. During the sixty-day term of the limited warranty, Course Technology will provide a replacement disc upon the return of a defective disc.

Limited Liability:

THE SOLE REMEDY FOR BREACH OF THIS LIMITED WARRANTY SHALL CONSIST ENTIRELY OF REPLACEMENT OF THE DEFECTIVE DISC. IN NO EVENT SHALL COURSE TECHNOLOGY OR THE AUTHOR BE LIABLE FOR ANY OTHER DAMAGES, INCLUDING LOSS OR CORRUPTION OF DATA, CHANGES IN THE FUNCTIONAL CHARACTERISTICS OF THE HARDWARE OR OPERATING SYSTEM, DELETERIOUS INTERACTION WITH OTHER SOFTWARE, OR ANY OTHER SPECIAL, INCIDENTAL, OR CONSEQUENTIAL DAMAGES THAT MAY ARISE, EVEN IF COURSE TECHNOLOGY AND/OR THE AUTHOR HAS PREVIOUSLY BEEN NOTIFIED THAT THE POSSIBILITY OF SUCH DAMAGES EXISTS.

Disclaimer of Warranties:

COURSE TECHNOLOGY AND THE AUTHOR SPECIFICALLY DISCLAIM ANY AND ALL OTHER WARRANTIES, EITHER EXPRESS OR IMPLIED, INCLUDING WARRANTIES OF MERCHANTABILITY, SUITABILITY TO A PARTICULAR TASK OR PURPOSE, OR FREEDOM FROM ERRORS. SOME STATES DO NOT ALLOW FOR EXCLUSION OF IMPLIED WARRANTIES OR LIMITATION OF INCIDENTAL OR CONSEQUENTIAL DAMAGES, SO THESE LIMITATIONS MIGHT NOT APPLY TO YOU.

Other:

This Agreement is governed by the laws of the State of Massachusetts without regard to choice of law principles. The United Convention of Contracts for the International Sale of Goods is specifically disclaimed. This Agreement constitutes the entire agreement between you and Course Technology regarding use of the software.